Five Questions
in Search of an Answer

also by David Stafford-Clark:

PSYCHIATRY TO-DAY
PSYCHIATRY FOR STUDENTS
WHAT FREUD REALLY SAID
MENTAL HEALTH MANUAL
AUTUMN SHADOW
SOUND IN THE SKY

DAVID STAFFORD-CLARK

Five Questions in Search of an Answer

Religion and Life:
Some Inescapable Contradictions

WITH AN EPILOGUE BY
PROFESSOR NINIAN SMART

Thomas Nelson & Sons Limited

Thomas Nelson and Sons Limited
36 Park Street London W1Y 4DE
PO Box 27 Lusaka
PO Box 18123 Nairobi
PO Box 21149 Dar es Salaam
77 Coffee Street San Fernando Trinidad

Thomas Nelson (Nigeria) Ltd
PO Box 336 Apapa Lagos

Thomas Nelson (Australia) Ltd
597 Little Collins Street Melbourne 3000

Thomas Nelson and Sons (South Africa) (Proprietary) Ltd
51 Commissioner Street Johannesburg

Thomas Nelson and Sons (Canada) Ltd
81 Curlew Drive Don Mills Ontario

This book first published 1970

Copyright © 1970 by David Stafford-Clark

Printed in Great Britain by Butler & Tanner, Frome

SBN 17 123018 3

For Dorothy:

In you I have found love
And the imagination of love
That I had lost.

'*Es irrt der Mensch, so lang er strebt*'
('Man errs until his strife is ended')
J. W. V. GOETHE, *Faust (Erster Teil)*

'Experience, from being lyrical,
will become tragic;
for what is tragedy but the conflict between
inspiration and truth' GEORGE SANTAYANA

'Also He hath set the world in their heart,
so that man cannot find out the work
that God hath done, from the beginning
even to the end' Ecclesiastes 3 : 11

Contents

Foreword	page	xi
1. The Nature of the Problem: Whatever Happened to the Love of God?		1
2. The Need to Believe: But How, in What?		23
3. Who is Jesus Christ, and Why is He?		65
4. If There be No God, How Then can I be a Captain?		87
5. Who's to Doom, When the Judge Himself is Dragged to the Bar?		117
Introduction to Appendices: A Word of Warning		139
1. Violence		141
2. Torture		150
3. Sex		155
4. Drugs		160
5. Time		165
6. 'If I Were a Carpenter...'		169
Epilogue by Professor Ninian Smart		174
Bibliography		179

Foreword

This book was written before, and deliberately independently from, the lectures which were to be derived from it. They were the Inaugural Series of Nelson Lectures, given at the University of Lancaster from 27 April to 1 May 1970, inclusive, in the Department of Religious Studies under the Chairmanship of Professor Ninian Smart, Professor in the University.

To him, and to Messrs Nelsons, I am indebted for the stimulus to write the book and give the lectures. But the ideas hereinafter expressed have taken half a lifetime to accumulate: throughout their presentation in this book the author must ask the reader to remember that for every idea there is a time of first encounter; and that, for every one of us, such first encounters possess an inherent significance: even where, like missing identity discs, their particular significance may survive their omission. Most of Chapter One would stand, for me, from 1935 to the present; Chapter Two belongs mainly to the decade 1945–55; Chapter Three to 1955–65; and the last two chapters span the last ten years.

For this exposition of them all, I alone am responsible.

Cyprus/London   D.S.-C.
March/April 1970

Acknowledgements

The author is grateful to the following for their kind permission to include quotations from the books indicated:

The Bodley Head Ltd: *The Cult of Power and Other Essays* and *The Wild Goose Chase* by Rex Warner; Cambridge University Press: *Man on His Nature*, the Gifford Lectures delivered by Sir Charles Sherrington; J. M. Dent & Sons Ltd: *Selected Critical Writings of George Santayana* Vol. I, edited by Norman Henfrey; Faber & Faber Ltd: *Four Quartets* by T. S. Eliot; Hamish Hamilton Ltd: *The Unquiet Grave* by Cyril Connolly and *The Royal Hunt of the Sun* by Peter Shaffer; The Penguin Press and Dr Anthony Storr: *Sexual Deviation* by Anthony Storr; The Society of Authors and Jonathan Cape Ltd: *Collected Poems* by A. E. Housman; Vallentine, Mitchell & Co. Ltd: *Creation and Guilt* by Ignaz Maybaum; Yale University Press: *Psychology and Religion* by C. G. Jung.

I

THE NATURE OF THE PROBLEM:

Whatever Happened to the Love of God?

God is said to be love. In all the major religions of the world, this extraordinary but infinitely valuable concept has found a place.

As the task of speaking to an audience gathered to hear the inaugural series of the Nelson Lectures for the Department of Religious Studies of Lancaster University loomed before me, no one was more keenly aware than I myself of my lack of scholarly qualifications for the job. The Department of Religious Studies deals, as its title would imply, with comparative theology, with the religions of the world, their origins, similarities, and differences: moreover, its leader, Professor Ninian Smart, is an expert upon Oriental religions, and particularly upon the early development and historical aspects of Hinduism and its schismatic derivative, Buddhism.

My acquaintance with the religions of the world is that of the traveller with few maps and ultimately fewer still convictions or traces of the wonderful, savage, terrifying territories through which he has wandered. Even in the religion with which I am least unfamiliar – Christianity – I have perhaps never been entirely orthodox, and am now almost certainly heretical. Moreover, modern theology alarms me almost as much as medieval theology has horrified and disgusted me. But perhaps my best qualification lies simply in this very lack of an orthodox theological background.

During the early formative years of my childhood, my parents were ostensibly at least conforming Methodists. The first church I attended was a Methodist chapel, and most of what I remember of it were the constantly tremulous, rhythmically quivering Parkinsonian hands of a silver-haired elderly gentleman who sang loudly and valuably in the choir; the incomprehensibility to me of much of the simple worship and ritual; my fascination with some of the hymn tunes and my boredom and distaste for others, together with a genuinely inquiring child's mind into the meaning of their words, the words of the prayers and texts and lessons which formed part of the service.

When I first went with my parents, and was very young, I was allowed to leave before the sermon, which I had guilelessly misheard and misunderstood as being called 'the serpent'. My parents were amused and indulgent about this, and for some time my mother used to leave with me to escort me home and prepare my father's lunch, the family Sunday dinner; a routine which, one way or another, went on until my brother and I were old enough and boorish enough, in our later adolescence, to be unlikely to have got up until it was ready. But even then Sunday lunch punctuated the week.

Shortly after I was considered old enough to make my own way home before the serpent, but not yet old enough to gain from hearing it, I had my first frightening and wholly gratuitous encounter with casual violence.* Tak-

* See Appendix One, page 141. I must have been about seven.

ing a short cut home through a back street of my home town in which were a number of small council houses, I was accosted by a small bully of about my own age and size, who took exception to my posh, dressed-up appearance. I remember the encounter with all the clarity of the distorted screen memories of childhood illuminated by intermittent recollection throughout a lifetime.

His opening words to me were uncompromising and aggressive:

'Where do you think you're going, posh little toff?'

'I – er – don't quite gather what you mean.'

An excuse for this improbably pompous remark can only be sought in the fact that I was the eldest son of articulate parents, and that my father, the first member of a profession in his family, valued education and cultivated speech very highly, and set an example which we all tried to follow consistently at home. My only brother, whom I was to learn to love dearly, deeply, and forever, was at that time only three, so I was really in the position of the erudite and precocious little boy, the only son conversationally, as it were, of an upper middle class family at the time. My rejoinder was ill-received.

'Well you're not going to get by, see?'

'Yes I am.' (Tears were humiliatingly close.) 'Please. . . . Let me go on my way. . . .'

'Try and make me, posh toff.'

I did.

Without another word I suddenly gave him a fierce push in the chest. Taken unawares, although his had been the opening gambit, he staggered backwards, tripped over the kerb from which I had stepped originally with the intention of avoiding him when he confronted me on the pavement, and fell down suddenly on his behind. Instantly he began to wail; probably largely as an immediate and spontaneous reaction to this entirely unexpected reversal of our roles. I was terrified, and ran on down the street towards its junction with the main road which led past the cemetery to my home, hearing behind me the sounds of continued lament mingled with imprecation, and over my assailant's cries the deeper and more fearful voice of an elder brother or perhaps a father warning me against ever being found in that area again.

It is not unduly fanciful to suppose that even as this brief affray was in progress, the voice of the preacher delivering the serpent was extolling the praises of God, and reminding his hearers that God is Love.

The pattern of that ignominious victory has been repeated more than once in my life, as in the lives of many others. It is perhaps the pattern to which the survivors in this world become accustomed, as one aspect of their survival. There is in it neither triumph, nor any sense of achievement; still less is it associated with any kind of love. It is part of the natural accident of survival: and I suppose for life's losers, the pattern is that of my tiny opponent. To be pushed out of the way, to fall down, to get hurt, to lose out, and to cry. As far as it goes, there is little love about that either.

But God is said to be love: and more than that, in three out of the five major religions of the world (placed carefully in alphabetical order, since this can best display my attempt at an impartial search for truth among them), Buddhism, Christianity, Hinduism, Islam, and Judaism, the central concept of God also includes his Fatherhood of all mankind. The God of the Jews is the Father, of his chosen people but also the loving Father, known or unknown, of all mankind. That same loving Father is the God of the Christians; and as Hebrew scholars as well as Christian Arabists have been keen and careful to point out, that loving and paternalistic provident figure is perhaps only the same God called by another name, as Allah, throughout Islam. Hinduism and Buddhism differ only in that, while love is an essential part of their concept of the nature of creation, that nature is not necessarily personal or in any way identified with humankind, although Buddha himself was of course a human prince at the beginning. As Ignaz Maybaum, one of the most eminent theologians of contemporary Jewry, has written:

> Buddhist civilization has no concept of history, and pre-supposes a reality which is not yet purged of Gods and Spirits as is Western civilization. Asian 'reality' is like a dreamland, as we see it in the drawings of Japanese and Chinese artists. In the tender lines and flourishes of these drawings, neither trees, stones, mountains, rivers nor the human figures among them have any contours. They have no existence of their own, but flow into each other to make up something which is really nothing at all, like the hub in the middle of a wheel. A wheel cannot be imagined without a hub, but the hub is merely the nothing without which the spokes of a wheel could not exist. In the Buddhist cosmos, sustained by the nothing as the spokes of the wheel are sustained by the hub, things and living beings are nothing in themselves; actions do not have a real purpose, everything is according to an aesthetically strict form, and everything in the social sphere is conduct and etiquette without moral justification. No one ought to cry out against cruelty perpetrated upon himself or upon others. Pain is unredeemable: and it has to be borne without reproach and bitterness. One cannot, here, love one's neighbour in the way in which the Hebrew Bible bids us love him, because one's neighbour is not discovered as a neighbour. Your fellow man is not 'like you', as the Bible says of

one's neighbour; he is *tat tvam asi* – identical with you, even as a grain of sand in a heap is identical with other grains of sand. It is this world on which the Mona Lisa smiles with an expression so successfully caught by Leonardo da Vinci: it is a cold, impassive smile, outwardly friendly but in truth cruel. It is the smile of the Buddha. Westerners, too, can of course learn to smile like that: but the moment that smile steals over their faces they cease to be Westerners. How near to each other Judaism, Christianity, and Islam are when viewed from the background of Buddhist civilization – because there is in it nothing at all of Judaism, Christianity, or Islam. Buddhist civilization is Asia: Europe, Western civilization, is of Jewish Christian and Islamic make.*

Accept that interpretation or not as you wish. It has been written, and the book from which it has been taken certainly deserves to be read. But, as I have said, I find the stuff of theology at best alarming, at worst horrifying. We can explore together why, in due course. Suffice it for the moment to say that medieval theology was concerned not simply with the intellectual waste of scholasticism, the disputations about angels on pinheads or needlepoints, but also with the fearful, savage, and almost unbelievably sadistic and masochistic tortures of the Inquisition, including strappado and squashation. I paused to elaborate on these in the lectures; I will spare them and the reader further elaboration here.† Vivid accounts of some of them can be found, for example, in Aldous Huxley's historical study, *The Devils of Loudun*; an account of the torture and execution of the priest who was believed to be the devil's agent after the sexual frustrations of the nuns, to whom he had ministered the sacrament, had escalated and exploded into hysterical and delusional accusations.

---

* Ignaz Maybaum, *Creation and Guilt*, Vallentine, Mitchell, London, 1969.
† See Appendix Two, page 150.

Modern theologians seem to me, however brilliant they may be, still to be like blind men stumbling about the interior of an incredibly ornate, beautiful, but desolate building: perhaps a church, perhaps a temple, perhaps a fortress, perhaps all three; or perhaps simply a place where people lived, or maybe still live. Unable to perceive its outlines or its plan, they make ground rules based upon the number of times they bark their shins; seeking order in what feels like chaos, and whose appearance they can never wholly see, they propound theories ostensibly scientific and illuminative, but actually finally incomprehensible and often self-contradictory. Seeking to fly up the stairs to the stars, they fall down them; and bravely limping on, mumble about where they have been, where their paths have crossed and why.

So I shall not pretend to refer except respectfully and in passing to people to whom I have from time to time been referred in the course of the kind of discussion into which a point of view such as mine inevitably leads its holder. Messrs Teilhard de Chardin, Paul Tillich, and Karl Barth are men who must be read to be appreciated, but to whom I have little to say in reply except, 'I wonder'. Barth can be briefly quoted, if only because he is perhaps the most poetic:

> Heaven is the creation inconceivable to man, earth the creation conceivable to him. He himself is the creature on the boundary between heaven and earth.

So much for the moment for complicated ideas. Suppose we consider a much simpler one, a hymn for children that I remember from the old days of the Methodist chapel and the serpent.

> All things bright and beautiful, all creatures great and small,
> All things wise and wonderful, the Lord God made them all.*

Within the context this meaning is perfectly clear and can be accepted as perfectly true. But, it must be added within the same context, presumably the Lord God also made the virus of poliomyelitis, the malaria parasite, the spirochete which causes syphilis, and the bacteria which causes tuberculosis, typhoid fever, and the innumerable other infections which have scourged, plagued, and destroyed mankind throughout history.

I write, as I hope I spoke, with humility; and from the particular standpoint of the doctor. A doctor whose life has been varied and whose experiences have been remarkably varied and abundant. 'Mortal man,' said Aldous Huxley, 'is avid of experience and counts all that he survives as gain.' As far as I know, I am, as I have admitted, a survivor. But I have begun to know something of the risks that survivors and losers alike must inevitably face. They do not seem to be distinguished particularly by a father's concern for his children, or God's infinite love for all his creatures.

Doctors are of course in no way bound to contest the truth of the statement that God is love; but their conception of what this statement means has to make room for what they know, as biologists, about the way life in the world is lived. We might make a start by considering one aspect of life which in sheer numbers of living creatures may well dwarf all terrestrial creation. I refer to life in the sea. It would appear to be a fact that fishes and other marine animals, in all forms at present recognized, are at

---

* Mrs Cecil Alexander (1812–95).

least 90 per cent carnivorous. Terrestrial animals are decidedly less so, although of course a large number of them live entirely by destroying and eating weaker and more vulnerable creatures. The sea, however, is particularly striking in this respect since it contains such enormous quantities of vegetation, which nevertheless provide food for only a very small proportion of the larger forms of marine animal life. Generally speaking, fishes of all sizes, shapes, and kinds live almost exclusively upon each other. Predatory destruction would seem to be the normal condition of life in the sea.

Biology has other and equally disconcerting lessons whose impact the doctor cannot avoid if he is to attain that honesty and objectivity which are indispensable to valid observation and deduction. He must recognize the existence, as part of the natural order of living creatures, of innumerable organisms which from the point of view of man and the larger animals are exclusively pathogenic. That is to say, they can only live by invading other creatures and partly or wholly destroying them. A large number of bacteria and viruses come into this category, as do protozoan parasites of the kind responsible for many tropical diseases such as malaria, amoebic dysentery, yaws, and sleeping sickness. The point about the agents of these diseases is that their entire life-cycle depends upon their creating havoc in their hosts. They have no other way of living, and yet they are most wonderfully and beautifully designed to sustain their life in these wholly and essentially destructive ways.

Bubonic plague, the Black Death of the Middle Ages, has more than once drastically cut back the world's population: now virtually extinct in Europe, it still occurs in widespread epidemics annually in India, with heavy mortality.

> Malaria [wrote Sherrington*] is the fever Homer told of. Only after the fifteenth century, when the great navigators had revealed the extent of the globe, did Europe begin to learn the extent to which this fever ravages the Earth. Today [1937–51] we know that in India alone it kills about 1,200,000 persons each year. For each person dying there are of course many ill. In some districts of India the entire population is ill with it. The quantity of human suffering and misery is beyond our actual appreciation. Nature has evolved in this plasmodium a means of inflicting pain and distress to an extent calculable but practically unimaginable. In that respect a dozen others of like kind compete with it for pre-eminence. It was in despair of Nature as any fountain-head for the moralist that Matthew Arnold wrote: 'Nature is cruel; man is sick of blood: Nature and man can never be fast friends.'
> In Hume's Dialogue the character Cleanthes offsets the pain to be found in Nature by co-existent equivalence of pleasure. Malaria is a chapter of biological knowledge new since Hume. What equivalence between pain and pleasure could Cleanthes trace there? Men, women, and children by the million suffering distress even to death. For what? To feed a thing not much unlike an amoeba of the pond, a protozoan parasite. Can we by any flight of fancy conceive that this speck of organized slime embodies a grain of pleasure? The mere suggestion, even if unwittingly, rings like a callous levity when heard against the groan of a tortured population.
> Naïve thought might suppose the scheme of Nature would at least value transcendence in life, e.g. a man more than a protozoan speck, or than a parasitic bacillus. But no. Of these latter that thrive by killing the former there are kinds too many even for mention here. There is, for one, that lowly and destructive life, the tubercle bacillus, which martyrs men and animals the habitable globe over. A hundred and thirty years ago John Keats, the poet, equally young and great, succumbed to it at the age of twenty-five. It had destroyed

* Sir Charles Sherrington, *Man on his Nature*, Penguin Books, Harmondsworth, 1955.

his lungs. Of his last book, the year before his death, there was said not long since by an exacting critic: 'The more I read it the more disposed am I to think this book to be, of all the world's books, upon the whole the most marvellous.' Keats had, in vain, nursed his younger brother attacked by that same venomous speck, and was in turn infected himself. The story is one of inexorable tragedy, nobly borne. Of Cleanthes' countervailing compensation is there any here? Fate in Greek tragedy was inexorable by divine nature. But here it is inexorable by mere chemistry. It is for man as critic and censor to interfere.

These venomous specks and others are sustained at cost of an immense sum of human suffering. To Hume's good Cleanthes the fact would doubtless be strange as distasteful. It seems truliest faced by recognizing that Nature, though she has evolved life, makes no appraisal of it. She has no lives of higher worth or of lower worth because to her all lives are without worth. If she is purely an assembly of mechanistic principles how should she appraise? Hume makes his character Philo inveigh against Nature 'pouring forth into her lap without discernment or parental care her maimed and abortive children'. Today [1951] a geneticist speaking of evolution tells us that the majority of oncoming mutations are lethal to their individuals. But to Philo's suggestion that Nature is immoral, today's reply is 'non-moral, not immoral'. Design or no design, some will say, and perhaps Hume would be among them, it is for man in reliance on his own dictates to take sides in this battle between life and life. Aristotle found in Nature 'unconscious purpose'. Read by evolution, Nature, now containing higher animal life and man, begins to contain a certain conscious purpose.

Sherrington was of course right. The Gifford Lectures, from which this passage is taken, were delivered in 1937 and 1938, and their published book was revised as recently as 1951. But exactly the prediction made by the author was to come to pass within the next twenty years, in a form very different from that which he had envisaged. Nature, now containing higher animal life and man, began to contain not only a certain conscious purpose; but somehow, as though inevitably within that purpose, the terrifying contradiction of man's colossal ingenuity and determination in exercising that purpose.

Ecology is that branch of science which deals with the natural order of things; the balance struck by nature uncontaminated by man's endeavours to force his own solutions upon it (or upon her, to remember for a moment Sherrington's almost flirtatiously condign assault by observation upon the pitiless processes of natural development). One of man's first targets, when he became able to meet nature on her own terms, was the eradication of the life-cycle of two of those chief enemies of whom Sherrington had written: the malaria parasite and the tubercle bacillus.

Since the tubercle bacillus could manage a life-cycle exclusively carried out within the human race, it had to be attacked directly and on its own ground. It was. The antibiotics designed to kill the tubercle bacillus were brilliantly successful, so that, whereas when Sherrington was writing there were sanatoria all over Europe and America for chronic but often slowly and remorselessly dying victims of tuberculosis, there are now virtually none. Instead, the tubercle bacillus has succumbed to a biochemical assault which appears, at least for the moment, to have totally vanquished it. Tuberculosis is no longer a scourge anywhere in the world where antibiotics are available, and the tubercle bacillus may well be on the way to final and complete extermination. Few will mourn its passing, fewer still will ask for natural reserves where it may be preserved as a kind of living museum specimen; although, as we shall also have occasion to see later, these natural reserves may be artificially maintained in the ceaseless search for methods of human destruction which form part of the chemical and bacterial warfare departments of most of the major powers. But unless they survive in these horrifying and man-made situations, tubercle bacillii are probably doomed.

The malaria parasite could probably be killed in exactly the same way: but its complicated life-cycle enabled man's ingenuity to devise an even more certain and seemingly biologically appropriate way of destroying it. Part of the life-cycle, it will be remembered, depends upon the parasite spending some time in the stomach and salivary glands of the anopheline mosquito. Exterminate the anopheline mosquito, and mankind could eliminate two pests for the price of one. The extermination of the mosquito could be undertaken by first spraying all stagnant pools and open water with a chemical such as DDT, which would kill the larvae of the mosquito. Even before DDT was available, in the earlier part of the Second World War, when the destruction of the anopheline mosquito held a high priority with the Western Allies, such pools in Asia were sprayed with paraffin so that the larvae could not come up to breathe. But this incidentally killed all the small fish in the small open pools used for both drinking and the cultivation of such fish, and called tanks throughout the Asian subcontinent. This effect had been predicted by Asian experts on the spot, to whom famine, as the consequence of the failure of crops or fishes – as it might be the very loaves and fishes of the parable – are an all too common event. Spray the tanks, said they, and you will kill the fish. Kill the fish, and you will precipitate the famine. May not that be a high price to pay for the destruction of mosquitoes all over

Asia? The answer was yes, it might seem that way at first at least, but the Allies could fly in food, whereas they could not allow malaria to ravage their supply lines and their personnel, and so at whatever cost the mosquitoes had to go.

In the event, famine in East Bengal certainly followed the first wave of spraying, and to use a common enough but perhaps doubtful phrase in this context, God alone knows what damage the chemical insecticides may have done by this time in their widespread use, not simply in wiping out the entire mosquito species, which had been marked down by man for destruction, but also in the mass spraying of crops to promote pest control and selective fertilization, even at the cost of mounting inclusion, in the fruits of those crops, of the very poisons used against the insect and ultimately lethal to man.

As I gave these lectures, ecologists all over the world were crying out for a pause in man's capacity to destroy his environment, possibly irretrievably, at least as far as he himself was concerned. When man emerges from Nature to tip her balance, he may find himself sawing off the branch from which he has all along been hanging. This sounds like a complicated feat, and indeed it is; but it is just as effective as the complicated analogy which it has evoked. It is as though what we have so often heard described as the God-given intelligence of human beings, once they were released to make significant changes in their environment, was too little controlled either by love or wisdom to avoid doing in the long run as much or even greater harm than in the short run it could do good.

Moreover, as a hunter, man's ingenuity has proved equally disastrous. Many animals are extinct and have become extinct in my lifetime, and many more are headed for extinction with helpless certainty if man continues to prey upon them with as little foresight as he preyed upon the North American buffalo, and even today is preying upon the spawning salmon and upon the whales of all the oceans of the world.

'God's in His Heaven, all's right with the world.' Or should that be amended to: 'God's in His Heaven, all was right with the world, until man began to try and improve on it.' But even if the second quotation did not contain an element of monstrous injustice, in that by no means all man's efforts to control disease, agony, and death in his environment have been totally without altruism; that injustice would be finally and ironically complete with the recognition that, if man upsets the balance of Nature by killing in order to save himself or line his pockets, killing, as a method of controlling, is one of Nature's favourite forms of maintaining her own mysterious and inexplicable balance: a balance of destruction that was to Sherrington, as indeed to any thinking and sensitive man, all too often totally hideous in its overall effects and their contemplation.

And so, with just these few examples, and leaving out so many other scourges, plagues, and natural disasters, we reach the first of the five questions posed by the nature of the problem.

Is Nature God's creature, if there is a God? And if the answer to that question is yes, how can that God be a loving God? Part of the question is answered with a kind of sardonic hopeless and yet positively assertive passivity, in a line from the Hindu hymn: 'All creation is the sport of my mad mother Kali.' Kali, the Hindu goddess of birth, of death, of sexual beauty, ecstasy, and corruption, of waste and filth, of carnage, wars, tyranny, and massacre. Kali, the goddess of life and death, who cares nothing for either but keeps the great natural cauldron bubbling with hate as well as with love. Is that the best answer we can find to the first question? If it is, can it possibly satisfy us, and is our quest either for satisfaction, or a better answer, itself an illusion?

That quest is certainly religious: any quest or question about the nature of reality is ultimately religious. But it was after turning such matters over in his mind that Freud came to his own inescapable conclusion that religion was an illusion, and drew unfortunately from that conclusion all the others which followed it and were set out in his book *The Future of an Illusion*.

I have dealt at sufficient length in another book with Freud's religious belief.* I will not repeat here what I said there, except simply to point out that this brilliant man's powerful attack upon the idea of a loving paternal God, and the system of religious beliefs and values surrounding him, was variable and multi-pronged. As much perhaps as anyone ever does, Freud knew what he was doing. Some of his metaphysical and philosophical arguments were decidedly shaky; but none of them were ill-considered. His explanation of the human conscience in terms of his concept of the super-ego, derived essentially from the child's reaction to earlier environment, and particularly to parental attitude and example, makes no provision for any inherent or absolute appreciation of right and wrong, and is in this sense independent fundamental religious or moral significance. There is nothing supernatural about religion in any of its forms, said Freud: and for him this conclusion

* David Stafford-Clark, *What Freud Really Said*, Macdonald, London, 1965.

carried considerable force. Indeed, he went on to treat the idea of God and the fact of religious belief as no more than projections of the child's relationship to his father, made in response to the wider stresses and threats of human existence, against which no human father could be expected to protect his son.

In essence Freud dismissed the idea of God as an illusion created by humanity to comfort them in the face of their helplessness when they had outgrown their parents. He ascribed their sense of guilt and shame to an original primitive act of murder, suggesting that the sons of a prehistoric tribe had rebelled against their father, killing him to gain possession of his women. Despite this explosive excursion into imaginative mythology, Freud believed and proclaimed that this thesis provided a rational basis to the abandonment of religion, while in the book already mentioned (*The Future of Illusion*) he concluded, frankly and reluctantly, that mankind was not yet ready for the challenge implied by this liberation from religious belief, but therefore the worship of God, and belief in an absolute system of values belonging to him, was a necessary fiction to preserve some semblance of law and order until the human race advanced sufficiently in wisdom to do without any of the illusions to which it had hitherto clung.

Throughout all this aspect of his writing, which has served to make many honest religious people deeply suspicious of psychology, and indeed of psychiatry too, and has underlain much of the misunderstanding which has surrounded Freud's work, Freud himself defended it vigorously. In fact, he tended to display an inflexible dogmatism about this aspect of his theory, which, had he encountered it in anyone else, would have suggested to him the strong possibility of an emotional rather than an objective scientific basis for its development. Indeed, if we permit ourselves the same speculations about him that he, much to our edification and instruction, has permitted himself about Moses and Leonardo da Vinci, we may wonder whether his own unresolved conflict and intensely charged feelings about his own father were not, perhaps, as much responsible for his views about conscience and religion, particularly as exemplified by the Jewish and Christian idea of a personal God, as were any of his scientific abilities.

Be that as it may, it remains true that Freud could claim no more authority for his conclusions than could be claimed for the subjective speculations of anybody else. His brilliant ability to explain the idea of God and the idea of Fatherhood might be linked in the human mind, and how both ideas could be expected to become involved in the developing conscience of the individual, is in no sense an answer to the very much wider and infinitely more important question of why the concept of God should be a part of human mental existence at all.

This, with perhaps an attempt at least at a partial answer, will be the subject of the second chapter and the second question. But while I was wrestling with it, I was reminded of two poems I had written, at two different stages of my life; part of four collections of poetry which represent one of my endeavours to seek, through the medium of art, a loving and viable alternative to the medium of science or even of logical disputation, in trying to grapple with this immense, immeasurably difficult, and perhaps ultimately logically insoluble problem.

The first poem was written just before the outbreak of

the Second World War, in the twenty-first year of my life. I think it worthy of preserving without further elaboration or explanation. A medical student of that age and in that time was to find much else to say on this topic:

MAYFLIES AT MONTAUBAN

>Over the bridge at Montauban
>The yellow lamps salute the sky,
>Dimly they mark the narrow span,
>Wink at the water sliding by;
>None would pretend that they light the way
>Or guide the stranger's stumbling tread,
>But a myriad mayflies own their sway
>For a few short hours, and then are dead.
>
>Held in the thrall of the dingy beam
>A numberless crowd of insects fly,
>Rising like wraiths from the Stygian stream,
>Rising – but only again to die.
>Tiny perfection of wing and limb
>And minutely delicate sentient brain –
>Where is the sense in Creation's hymn
>When life's wonder is squandered in death and pain?

The second poem was written about ten years later, when I was in America, on a post-graduate fellowship, in the course of gathering together knowledge and experience in that branch of medicine in which I have since spent the greater part of my life.

Just before conceiving the idea of this poem I had been living, somewhat sparsely, in International House in Chicago – a hostel for post-graduate students distinguished more in the conception of the underlying idea than the provision of any physical comfort. Nevertheless, compared to many of the peripheral dwellings of Chicago, itself a rough, rich, violent, and frightening city, built in places with a careless beauty and in others with an almost indescribable seediness and waste, it was paradise.

I had spent time there reflecting on the human predicament, which is after all only the ultimate anguish of the predicament of all life: ultimate, because more aware. Man, unlike all other animals, is a creature that 'can look before and after . . .'. By that is meant a creature who knows that life existed before him and will continue after him; and is thus given a glimpse of at least the possibility of transcendent good or evil. But although he can conceive both what is wholly good and what is avoidably bad, in the way in which the world runs, and the living creatures in it, yet he is also bound to realize that his own instincts and his own needs are at war with his aspirations towards such goodness. Moreover, this is a war which divides all the forces of instinctual life, remorselessly and totally. As we have seen, animal life cannot continue except by destroying other lives; whether the life of other and less powerful animals, or of plants. The price of life itself is in fact waste, cruelty, and destruction as human beings see them; just as the rewards of life can include love, beauty, and wonder. If I repeat these points, it is only because they must never be forgotten.

I had not forgotten them when I wandered into Chicago's Museum of Modern Art, and saw there on the wall an Indian-ink line-drawing of powerful impact, of a winged horse crushed beneath the wreckage of a shattered building. I looked at the name of the artist: it was typed on a small slip attached to the bottom of the picture and I have forgotten it. But added was the information that the artist was a Polish citizen, a member of the British Airborne

Forces during the Second World War, whose emblem was Pegasus, the winged horse. The poem which crystallized my visual experience on seeing this remarkable drawing is concise, deliberately allegorical, but aimed at illuminating both the predicament of life, and the paradox whereby the God of love can also be a God of suffering and death:

PEGASUS

I am the prisoner
And beyond the bars, I am the man
Striding the distant hill;
Seeing the prison's boundary, feeling the cold
Thrust in the heart; fearing imprisonment,
Sharing the prisoner's grief, the prisoner's torment.

Man who torments all creatures and himself
Needs always pity; fighting and hating
Man needs love: Yet who but God
Can bear to love him, and to let him suffer.

All earth is wrung with helpless cries
That few can hear; that few can bear to hear
The plunging whale, grappled to a wire
Seals stripped and bleeding on the icy shore.
The beaver choked below his shattered dam
The hunter hunted and slayer slain
Man in his pride and certainty confounded
Betrayed by ruthlessness and numbed by pain.

Horse with the broken wings
Crouching beneath the girders
Forelegs fashioned to outsoar the stars
Pinions to span the sky
Now sprawling under iron
Barbed wire and concrete of captivity.

All are to blame: there is no innocence but birth
No guilt but pride, no debt but love
And no reward but loving. All our agony

And all our joy, mean only this.
Out on the battlements
The maimed doomed horse
Crouches below the sightless stars
But in his darkening eyes
Soars still the wild brave vision
Image of winged horse against the sky.

2

THE NEED TO BELIEVE:

But How, in What?

The doctor and the priest are concerned, each in his own way, with man's needs. One of these is the need to believe. Man is not, and cannot be, content to accept life as meaningless. Even when stridently proclaiming a materialist philosophy which inexorably robs his existence of ultimate meaning or purpose, man continues, despite himself, to behave as though what he did mattered. Indeed, to proclaim a philosophy at all, or hold a point of view, inevitably implies an underlying assumption that there is a meaning in life.

Even the most base philosophies, the most degraded concepts of society, cannot entirely escape the necessity of postulating some sort of purpose for their justification. The priest is certain of the purpose, and when the doctor refuses to acknowledge a personal attitude towards it at all, he is merely taking refuge in an agnosticism which is not supported by his own study of the intensely purposeful nature of biological and physiological processes. In one sense, both doctor and priest are bound to be confronted with this question of purpose, and perhaps the psychiatrist as a special kind of doctor has a particular contribution to make to this problem.

Psychiatry is one of the ways by which men seek to understand themselves; its special province is understanding the life of the mind, and particularly the sick mind; but it is bound to concern itself fundamentally with the basic needs and drives which move through the mind, in health as in sickness.

Psychiatry therefore is confronted by a number of such basic needs and drives; and has tended in the past to accept some of them less critically than others.

The sexual instinct, the instinct of self-preservation, the drive towards power, and the need to love which, if thwarted, becomes the urge to hate – all these have been accepted in their own right; but somehow psychiatry has always had more difficulty in accepting the need to believe as equally profound or important. Yet careful and objective study of man's life reveals him in search, not only of immediate physical satisfactions, but, beyond these, in search of some sort of point and purpose in living at all. This search may take many forms, and may be conscious or unconscious, constant or fluctuating, but it is an inescapable aspect of human existence. Blake and Kafka saw it as the ultimate quest and almost certainly as the real reason for temporal existence itself.

There are at least some grounds for believing that this purpose is part of a design which can be recognized in the whole of existence, and at this point it must be frankly admitted that for some people this belief has the quality of knowledge. This knowledge can be called 'awareness', meaning by this awareness, not understanding of the real nature of existence, not insight or revelation into the true purpose and design referred to above, but simply acknowledgement that such purpose and design exist, and that all else exists only through and because of them. Such a postulate demands ultimately and inevitably a belief in God – without, however, necessarily illuminating much further the individual's idea of what God is like. So far only will logic and reason take man, but this is far enough indeed to awaken in him the fundamental need to seek further: to strive to discover the nature of this ultimate reality from which are derived the purpose and design of existence; to discover, moreover, if he can, his own relationship to this reality and what it implies.

The attitude of psychiatry towards this need tends to be dominated by the personal and emotional necessities of the particular psychiatrist; perhaps the best-known example being that of Freud himself. I have referred briefly to some of his views in Chapter One of this book, and dealt at greater length with them in another.* Freud's criticism of religion has been described as a criticism of the wish-fulfilment aspect of religion; believing because it is more comfortable to believe, because such a belief implies a promise of pie in the sky when you die. The popular version of this theory is a peculiarly superficial one. It entirely ignores the fact that the central idea of religion is not a projection of gratification, but a quest: a quest for the purpose of life, and for the individual's place in this purpose; a quest for a relationship in which men can give rather than receive. Worship, not reward, is the consistent feature of the great religions of the world.

Quite apart from particular attitudes of this kind, there has for long been the curiously naïve assumption on the part of many psychiatrists that it is somehow unscientific to acknowledge the reality of a need whose satisfaction

* David Stafford-Clark, *What Freud Really Said.*

cannot be completely explained or guaranteed by scientific methods. But this need is not only undeniable; the attempt to deny it inevitably leads to an even more violent assertion of the natural demand, most of all in the minds of those who have neither acknowledged it nor consciously sought its fulfilment.

What happens when men attempt to abolish the idea of God in a society for which they are responsible has been succinctly described by Rex Warner:*

> ... The more successful the moral anarchists are, the greater is the feeling of uncertainty in the minds of everyone, including in the end the moral anarchists themselves.... There is one way of escape for the leader, and that is by giving to the mass of the people, what they want – a system of ideas by which they can regulate and give meaning to their lives. (Indeed this is something which, by this time, the leader needs himself.) But the old idols are smashed and to resuscitate them would be to admit failure. There is only one thing for it – after having rejected God to make himself God, and to cause it to be generally believed that those characteristics by which he won his first eminence – and perhaps these have been self-assertion, violence, brutality, amongst others – are the characteristics of Godhead. The old faith, the old system of values, must have been very thoroughly disintegrated to make such a plan possible....

Such disintegration periodically occurs, and may be the breeding-ground for Fascism in the community where it has happened. Germany in 1935 is a tragic but classic example. The whole idea behind Fascism is that of the privileged élite; inherently superior, 'not as other men are', in contrast to whom the rest of the community exist only on

* Rex Warner, *The Cult of Power*, John Lane, The Bodley Head, London, 1946.

sufferance, to provide scapegoats or be exploited. No further or more extreme denial of the brotherhood of man, or of the concept of God as a loving father in whose sight all men are of equal (and infinite) value, can be imagined. Fascism has neither time nor room for theism.* The same idea can be traced in the approach of perhaps the most famous psychiatric philosopher of all: Jung. He has written:

> The gods first lived in superhuman power and beauty on the top of snow-clad mountains or in the darkness of caves, woods and seas. Later on they drew together into one God, and then that God became man. . . .

Jung goes on to observe what happens when man seeks to make a purely scientific approach to this problem:

> At first the materialistic error seems to be inevitable; since the throne of God cannot be discovered among the galactic systems, the inference is that God has never existed. The second inevitable mistake is psychologism. If God is anything He must be an illusion derived from certain motives, from fear for instance, from will to power, or from repressed sexuality. These arguments are not new. Similar things have already been said by the Christian missionaries who overthrew the idols of the pagan gods. But whereas the early missionaries were conscious of serving a new God by combatting the old ones, modern iconoclasts are unconscious of the one in whose name they are destroying the old values. . . .

If a man seeks to dispose of the idea of God, says Jung,

> . . . then he should find out at once where this considerable energy which was first invested in an existence as great as God, has disappeared to. It might reappear under another name, it might call

---

* However, the élite must band together to stay on top; hence the 'fasces' (Latin word for bundle) as their classic emblem of inviolable supremacy.

itself 'Wotan' or 'The State' or something ending with -ism, even atheism, of which people believe, hope, and expect just as much as they formerly did of God.

... If dull people lose the idea of God nothing happens – at least not immediately and personally. But socially the masses begin to breed mental epidemics, of which we now have a fair number [c. 1933–4].*

The psychological truth of this need to believe can be defended from many other sources, by no means all of them religious. But this need to believe carries with it its own inescapable difficulties; it confronts men with the need to make an act of faith in a God whose immediate presence is not apparent.

God may be presented to men either as a religious concept, or as a direct experience, a mystical revelation of the nature of God himself; an experience denied to many who none the less achieve their act of faith through the acceptance of a revealed religion. Such an act of faith is a step which some who encounter it are not prepared to take. Of these a number simply shrink from acceptance and thereby condemn themselves to lives uninspired by any fundamental creed or philosophy at all; others, conscious of an overwhelming need to believe in something but unable to accept either the idea of God or the uncompromising reality of spiritual values unalterable by expediency and transcending even the highest human endeavours, turn to dialectical materialism or the philosophical aspects of psychoanalysis† for their consolation. They succeed in this way in satisfying their need to believe – at least for the

---

* C. G. Jung, *Psychology and Religion*, Yale University Press, 1946.
† Freud's three classical monographs are *The Future of an Illusion*, *Civilisation and its Discontents*, and *Moses and Monotheism*, and these form the bibliographical foundation. See *What Freud Really Said*.

time being. But to the Christian their respective creeds, as substitutes for a central awareness and acceptance of God, are disastrous illusions, as inevitably foredoomed to tragedy and failure as was the Tower of Babel. If God exists, there can be no substitute for him. If he does not, existence itself is without ultimate meaning.

This is not Christian propaganda. It is an inescapable fact. The modern version of existentialism starts from this as a premise, and being essentially atheist, is therefore inevitably pessimistic to the point of despair. Logical positivists have dealt with it simply by begging the entire question of the significance of the concept of ultimate meaning. But to deny significance to ideas because they are beyond the scope of logical proof or disproof is to ignore fundamental psychological considerations. As Jung pointed out, there is no greater idea in the mind of man than the idea of God, whatever form this idea takes, and to dismiss such a tremendous concept as meaningless is deliberately to side-step reality as presented to us in any study of man's behaviour.

Side-stepping of this kind is impossible for the Christian because he cannot remain unaware of man's emotional predicament. Man needs to believe in something intangible, and it is just the inescapable reality of this need which drives him to become an existentialist or a logical positivist, or a Communist, or a Christian.

Of the four examples selected, the Christian differs from the other three in this way: he acknowledges his need to believe as something implanted in him from without. Furthermore, he accepts the need as logical and inevitable in itself, since for him the ultimate object of belief is one with the source of all reality. The other three disciplines share a contrasting task: they have to invent the source of their own belief before they can accept it; and it always remains for them the product of their own invention, having no other source. If they are right, then the Christian is certainly wrong. But if they are right then rightness itself ceases to have any absolute meaning, being merely a convention of human thought. The passion with which they will defend this ultimately meaningless concept of their rightness is yet further vivid evidence of the emotional necessity of belief.*

Man therefore has an overwhelming need, which a psychiatrist cannot afford to ignore but which he cannot pretend to be able to satisfy. Has psychiatry therefore nothing to contribute to this problem? In one sense it certainly has, because one of the essential tasks of psychiatry is to understand the patient's needs and to open the way to his own understanding of them. In this way the patient can be enabled to solve his own problems, in the light of the insight into their nature which he has gained. And since the particular needs which psychiatry aims primarily to understand are mental rather than physical, it is especially concerned with those conditions in which human emotions, attitudes, and beliefs have been altered or disturbed by illness or adversity.

Minds, of course, can be as distorted by sickness as bodies, and their functions can suffer and become as crippled and as painful. C. S. Lewis has given a most helpful analogy to illustrate this particular point. He has likened the mind and body to a radio set, itself a compli-

---

* '... convinced materialists are ready to worship their own jerry-built creations as though they were the Absolute...' Aldous Huxley, *The Devils of Loudun*.

cated, delicate, but highly vulnerable piece of mechanism, tuned to receive a programme broadcast from a long way off. In conventional terms the set, even in its most complex and intricate design, is essentially 'material'; the programme, on the other hand, is essentially 'immaterial'. Yet the programme provides the ultimate justification for the existence of the set, and it is to receive and give expression to this programme that the set has been designed and built. None the less if the set becomes damaged or decayed, it is quite likely to distort the programme even to the point at which interference renders it no longer recognizable at all. At this point the set needs attention, although it may appear to the superficial listener that it is the programme which has gone wrong.

I have developed this analogy in my own words, because it has a particular use for the thesis of this chapter. In this use the psychiatrist must assume the role of the radio technician, and may be able to restore the set to something like working order; and in this sense he is working in harmony with the general purpose implicit in the full reception and reproduction of the programme, but he is not necessarily in better touch with the programme or its source than anybody else. A radio technician who takes upon himself the status of programme director or critic is clearly mistaking the limitations of his own capacity, at least in so far as these are bound up with his trade.

Modern psychiatry has learnt to consider mind and body as aspects of the same single phenomenon; this can be illustrated in innumerable ways, but recognition of the role of integration in the functioning of the endocrine, autonomic, and central nervous system connections, all of which serve to reflect the effects of emotions and bodily changes each upon the other, provides a most satisfactory method of exemplifying the fundamental nature of this relationship. Full acceptance of this relationship in turn makes easier acceptance of the wider and even more important integration between spirit, mind, and body which is demanded by an understanding of the true nature of man. This trinity of spirit, mind, and body can be regarded from a religious standpoint as being a mysterious union which lasts for the physical lifetime of an individual.

During this lifetime, while spirit is the ultimate essence of man, the part of him which is immortal and which reflects the supernatural element in his being, mind provides the opportunity for awareness, the means whereby he makes conscious contact with the everyday world around him, and the appearance of reality which this world represents; body is then the instrument whereby man makes physical contact with his environment, his stake in mortal existence, and the source of both the pleasure and the pain which are inseparable from human life.

Seen this way, the concept of the whole man takes on a completeness which no other way of regarding human existence can provide. This concept is both scientifically and spiritually compatible with the observable evidence. But while it is helpful in reconciling our understanding of these varied aspects of man, of itself it does nothing to reconcile them to each other. That they need some sort of reconciliation seems undeniable.

One of the most constant observations of all the various schools of thought in modern psychology is that man is perpetually experiencing conflict at both conscious and unconscious levels. Examination of any human problem can indeed be profitably undertaken only if these various and potentially conflicting aspects of man are fully acknowledged. That they are interrelated, and that tension and stress at any level produce repercussions throughout all these aspects, is another undeniable aspect of human experience. It remains to be seen what are the possible contributions of psychiatry to religion, and of religion to psychiatry, in these terms, and what are the pitfalls which both must avoid if they are not to mislead their followers into needless strife and antipathy.

We saw at the beginning of this chapter that the priest and the doctor are both concerned with man's needs. But they are not only concerned, they are pledged to minister to them, although in essentially different ways. These ways are however complementary, in just the same sort of way that the interrelationship of spirit, mind, and body is a complementary one.

The first task of the priest is to minister to man's spiritual needs – including the need to believe and the need to love, already recognized by the psychiatrist – by helping to bridge the gap between seeing and believing, between the reality of God and the possibility of man's acceptance of him. He may do this by faith and works, precept and example, love and leadership in a thousand spheres: but barring miracles his opportunities will inevitably be influenced by the state of mind of the man whom he seeks to help and win. A madman may be rigidly insusceptible – incapable of belief, or convinced that, for example, he is himself Jesus Christ.* At a less spectacular level, the dependence and immaturity of a neurotic patient may lead

* See Milton Rokeach, *The Three Christs of Ypsilanti*, Alfred A. Knopf, New York: Random House, Toronto, 1967.

him to demand from religion an idealized substitute for an all-indulgent parent, and then to reject God because his personal human problems are not immediately abolished by accepting the idea of him.

The task of the psychiatrist, as of any other doctor, is essentially to relieve suffering at the human level for as long as possible, to prevent it when it can be prevented, and to treat it by whatever means are available when it cannot. His immediate concern is with mental and physical anguish: but he will inevitably encounter spiritual conflict and distress just as the priest will come to grips with sickness and pain.

How then can they, and must they, contribute to one another's tasks? And what light does the answer to this question throw upon their relationship to one another as a whole?

Psychiatry can often cure or relieve insanity, no matter what form this takes; but quite apart from its function in the treatment of gross mental illness, it can help to clear the mind of emotional prejudices and conflict neither fully understood, acknowledged, nor consciously evaluated by the individual. By an extension of this process it can bring about a clarification and sharpening of man's approach to values and can sometimes increase his insight and awareness in dealing with controversial issues of all kinds – including religious problems. To return for a moment to the analogy of the radio set, the psychiatrist as a technician can immensely improve the clarity, sharpness, and definition of reception of the programme: that is, he can awaken and increase awareness and understanding, and thus often improve the stability and flexibility of the individual mind.

Apart from this, the therapeutic and humane exertions

of psychiatry, like those of any other branch of medicine, can play a part in easing suffering. One might sum this up by saying that any success achieved by psychiatry in straightening out a tangled mind, in helping a man to think more clearly and honestly, must inevitably help him also to open his mind and his heart to God – if he so chooses.

The contribution which Christianity can make to problems arising out of the therapeutic situation is fundamental. It can reconcile the inevitable conflict between loving and hating which psychotherapy may bring up into consciousness. It is important to realize that psychiatry by itself cannot really do this; it is not in itself a source of inspiration nor can it provide a substitute for moral values or obligations, and it is only inviting trouble to pretend that it can. Nor in this context can we disregard the inevitable failure of psychiatry, comparable again to the inevitable failure of any other branch of medicine, finally to avert suffering, catastrophe, or death. There are many situations in which human skills and even human compassion and concern are not enough to enable a patient to deal successfully with suffering. At this point the strictly natural levels of a man's being may be transcended.

Most important of all, Christianity can supply the ultimate purpose, the ultimate hope and the ultimate standard of values for human society as a whole; it is the one answer to the human need to believe which both explains and justifies this need; and for medicine and psychiatry, particularly in their ethical aspects, Christian standards remain indispensable. Without such standards, there is the ever-present danger of purely technical interests or apparent expediency subordinating recognition of the essential worth and dignity of man. Examples of this are the experiments on human beings in the concentration camps of the Second World War, and the recurrent popular suggestion that 'incurable lunatics' should be 'painlessly put away'.*

But despite their common ground and complementary goals, all too often there arise bitter conflicts between the priest and the psychiatrist, which, when they are not primarily personal, rest upon avoidable error, and are therefore unnecessary. There may be on the priest's part a dogmatic and misconceived opposition to certain aspects of psychiatry; for example, to hypnosis, on grounds that it 'weakens the will'; or to psychoanalysis, because of the philosophical implications of the subject, which can in fact be entirely separated from its practice as a therapeutic technique without any essential diminution in the latter's effectiveness. It is comparatively uncommon to see this separation in practice: but this is only because Christian analysts are themselves rare birds. Nevertheless, it remains true that the effectiveness of psychoanalysis in treatment depends essentially upon the nature and quality of the transference, and upon its skilful management. This is fundamentally an emotional relationship, and may be entirely independent of the theoretical views of the participants.

Indeed, as we have already seen, in most of the basic personal problems uncovered by the procedure of psychoanalysis, the Christian ethic has a far more positive contribution to make than could conceivably be offered by

* More recent disenchantment following all the lamentable ballyhoo over major transplant surgery led to one comment that all it seemed actually to amount to as yet was two deaths for the price of one.

Freud's own somewhat arid formulation. The importance of disinterested love in any form of psychotherapy is profound, and often incalculable. A better understanding of the nature of the various forms of psychiatric technique, an understanding which it is a duty of any Christian to acquire before he makes assertions about their moral aspects, would do much to prevent such conflict from arising.

Another and equally misconceived source of conflict arises when an attempt is made to equate the analytic couch with the confessional: this ignores the fact that, whereas it is the function of confession to deal with conscious guilt about voluntary and deliberate wrongdoing by asking God's forgiveness for admitted sins, the procedure of analysis is essentially concerned with bringing into awareness hitherto repressed unconscious feelings and with involuntary fantasies more often than with frank intentions or actual deeds. The two are therefore fundamentally different: indeed, the originator of the concept of the unconscious mind, with all its psycho-dynamic implications of magical thinking, infantile equation of the thought with the deed, repression of unmanageable or unbearable memories so that even the recollection of their existence is obliterated from consciousness, was Freud himself. Much of what Freud really said was directed towards demonstrating the fundamental fallacy of regarding conscious and unconscious mental life as in any way directly comparable.

An example of this fallacy in action is the equation of impulse and intention: this is sometimes achieved by over-scrupulous scholiasts in their interpretation of Matthew 5 : 28: '. . . whosoever looketh on a woman to lust after her hath committed adultery with her already in his heart'.

If this is taken to mean that the intention to commit adultery unopposed by conscience is scarcely less sinful than the commission of the act itself, the true sense of the passage is clear; but sometimes the argument is advanced that the mere experience of temptation in this direction is as bad as the act itself; people then are encouraged to feel guilty because they experience the normal temptations which are an inevitable part of the human situation.* It is a strange and ironic paradox that, apart from over-scrupulous priests and penitents, the only other source of this particular error is to be found in the general unconscious judgement of the Freudian super-ego, which it is the object of psychoanalysis to mitigate. To make this equation consciously, therefore, is to carry over into conscious thinking the primitive over-simplification characteristic of unconscious mental processes. It is in fact this very primitive and irrational quality of super-ego judgements which render them so demonstrably inadequate as a complete basis for conscience as a whole.

The ultimate source of morality, as of conscience, is spiritual and absolute – not merely the distilled or distorted relics of infantile experience and environment. Parental moral influence itself can only derive from the parents' own conscience in action, and the problem of its origin is shelved rather than solved by attributing the whole of one generation's morality to the conduct of their parents. We reflect what is in us as well as what has been done to us.

The opposite error to the application of unconscious,

* See Appendix Three, page 155.

primitive standards to conscious and complicated problems, is the attempt to apply the critical standards of every-day conscious life to the products of unconscious mental activity: this happens when patients with obsessional illnesses are led by over-zealous but misguided priests into extreme scruples or interminably obsessional confessions: or when visions and ecstasies which are in fact symptoms of intoxication or developing mental illness are accepted as supernatural manifestations.*

The cardinal error of which the psychiatrist is apt to be guilty in his approach to Christianity is implicit in the cult of 'psychologism' – in the attempt to explain away both the idea of God and the idea of evil – already discussed a little while back. This error leads inevitably to the necessity of creating new standards in place of those which have been destroyed, and ultimately replacing the idea of God by theoretical and somewhat arid rationalist proposals, which in the end come to rely upon the lowest elements in human conduct – such as treachery, brutality, and ruthlessness – for their upholding.†

Another red herring, which by this time has begun to go stale, is the postulate that modern psychology rests upon a determinist and materialist basis and that therefore, if it is valid, it constitutes in itself an argument for a determinist and materialistic basis to human existence. This proposition dates back to the pre-relativity period in physics, when determinism seemed empirically unassailable. Since absolute determinism has now everywhere been abandoned as a scientific hypothesis, modern psychology can no longer be said to rest solely upon it. Nevertheless modern

* See Appendix Four, page 160.
† See Rex Warner quotation, page 26.

physics remains deterministic, even though statistical, and neither supports nor denies the existence of free will in a human being. In so-called classical physics it was assumed that if full knowledge existed of the positions and velocities of all particles making up a system at a given moment, then all future states of the system could be forecasted. This was what Laplace meant when he said that in his universe '*il n'y à pas besoin de Dieu*'. The unfortunate fact is of course that you cannot know all the positions and velocities, and so Laplace's proposition fails. In modern physics, use is made of uncertainty principles, statistics, probabilities, wave equations and the like, but determinism is by no means abandoned, nor is the entrance of free will into the human being thereby facilitated.

For a detailed and vivid refutation of the fundamentally materialist determinist attitude to the study of man, the reader can turn to Professor C. S. Lewis, Professor V. H. Mottram, Kenneth Walker, and most recently Dr Seaborn Jones;* all of whose books deserve attention on their own merits.

Priests and psychiatrists, therefore, do not have to disagree: there is so much else for them to do. In our essentially fragmentary and imperfect view of life and living there is apparent through all the conflict and confusion a consistent theme and a transcendent mystery. It would seem that pain, guilt, failure, and ultimately death, are in some way inevitable aspects of the human situation. They may be mitigated by medicine, but man cannot completely escape from them, nor would he be the same creature, with the same opportunities, vision, and possibilities, if he could.

Atonement, forgiveness, love, and redemption are

* See Bibliography for recommended reading.

similarly an essential part of the divine answer to the human predicament. They are the complementary aspects to the hopelessness of humanity by itself. There is in fact an inevitability of failure, at the purely human level, balanced by an abiding possibility of redemption through love, at the divine level, which man needs and which he is bound to seek. As I have already ventured to say in another place,* there is nothing about a belief in psychiatry which makes impossible a belief in God; and nothing about a belief in God which makes impossible a belief in psychiatry. The part is not greater than the whole.

But even so, we cannot spare ourselves the question as to what is the real aspect of this whole from which we seek to rend some substance for our belief. All our values certainly depend upon some ultimate concept of absolute value, which has so often in the past been taken as being directly provided by God's purpose and his ultimately divine reality. We have begun to dare to question this purpose, at least in so far as it can be made comprehensible in human terms: we must go on to examine also some further manifestations of the way in which it is worked out in practice. God, it must certainly seem, cannot simply be a divine extrapolation from Nature. If that were true, God could not simply be love, he would have to be like Kali, the supremely omnipotent, but equally supremely indifferent, arbiter of all creation. He could not be the loving Father of mankind. He would not be fit to be a father as we have learned to know, value, and idealize that concept, even at a human level. This extraordinary gulf between the image, and what can be inferred of the actuality, in terms of the human predicament, seems to

* *Psychiatry To-day*, Penguin Books, Harmondsworth, 1952.

obsess, among others, the writer Samuel Beckett. Aware of it he certainly is, and has striven for years to compel a comparable awareness in his readers and audiences. The emergent message has a recurrent ring of hopelessness: yet hopelessness itself is not a message, and in itself provides no motive for attempting to convey one. But, while he lives, Beckett does not cease from mortal strife . . . in fact he goes on writing.

Leaving aside God's paternal responsibilities for a moment, how does he shape up as an architect and designer? Bernard Shaw once quoted Helmholtz as declaring that 'the eye has every possible defect that can be found in an optical instrument and even some peculiar to itself' – and further, that 'if an optician tried to sell an instrument which had all these defects, I should think myself quite justified in blaming his carelessness in the strongest terms, and sending him back his instrument'.

Whether or not Helmholz's indictment of the eye is regarded as a justifiable criticism of the technical construction and design of an instrument for seeing, there can of course be no doubt that other instruments even nearer to the seat of consciousness, perhaps most of all the brain, represent marvels of efficiency and compactness. Nevertheless, the method of reproduction and growth in the developing human organism, following fertilization of the ovum, are beset with complicated sequences leading to the final production of the various bodily organs; sequences of processes which can and do fail. When such a failure occurs in the course of development, the results are congenital deformity and disability, mental and physical, which precede the birth of the individual and may remain as lifelong and sometimes terribly crippling disabilities.

BUT HOW, IN WHAT?

In many instances the errors which occur, and the long-term and cumulative effects which follow them as the result of later processes being unable to reach a satisfactory stage of completion because the initial stages have gone wrong, correspond precisely to what might be seen at the end of a production line in a factory where a process or mechanical operation had gone wrong at an early stage, and the effects of this initial error had piled up and increased in exactly the way they would were the process neither halted nor corrected. But there is of course this difference: the production line in a factory can be halted, inspection can occur at each and every stage along the line, and a faulty or defective part can be removed and replaced before the finished article can reach the end in a hopelessly damaged or distorted condition. Unfortunately, none of these saving operations are as yet possible in the case of living organisms, and perhaps least of all in human beings, whose evolutionary development in the womb, from single cell to full mature individual, is the most complicated of all. By the time a baby is born, after nine months of remarkably intricate development, processes can have gone wrong which result in distortions and deformities by this time quite irremediable, and often piteously severe.

So that while the doctor may indeed marvel at the intricacy and relative perfection of detail of the human body in its normal development, and in its full maturity of structure and function, he must also deplore the apparent mechanical crudity whereby a small error at an early stage in intra-uterine life cannot be corrected once it is established, but must inevitably pile up a chaos which results in deformity or defect of an irremediable kind. In this connection one might pose a question and attempt an answer:

Q: Is an idiot or a mongol or a hydrocephalic monster created in the image of God?
A: Presumably, yes: but the image of God imprisoned in imperfect, but by no means necessarily individually guilty, flesh.

For so wonderful a design, a process so readily capable of developing flaws seems somehow clumsily inappropriate.

There are other ways in which the same apparent contradiction between wonder of design, and yet mechanically avoidable imperfection in operation, occurs. The body contains a number of cyclical mechanisms in its normal working which constitute inherent potential flaws. They are capable of becoming vicious circles if their balance is disturbed. Most examples of these would require perhaps more detailed medical knowledge than can be offered at this point for their full understanding, but a simplified illustration is provided by the response of the delicate tubular tissue of the kidneys to a prolonged increase in blood pressure. There is considerable evidence that the kidneys can be damaged by a sustained increase in blood pressure, but also that their normal internal control mechanism contains elements which tend to raise blood pressure if they have been damaged, since a damaged kidney requires a relatively greater rate of blood flow through it to continue to work efficiently. This provides a perfect example of a vicious circle which tends to become fatal, since the damaged kidney pushes up the blood pressure to a degree which ultimately increases the damage to itself and its fellow. And once the kidneys are irretrievably damaged, death inevitably follows. This is only one example of many.

In fact all the most important organs in the human body, such as the liver, the kidneys, the heart, and the brain, while possessing vast but necessarily limited reserves, are characterized without exception by being exceedingly vulnerable to damage from oxygen lack or infection: by being completely indispensable to continued existence; and finally by being quite irreplaceable. This has always limited medicine to a crucial extent, and together with the fact that doctors have no finally authoritative blueprint to show them how the human body was designed or is supposed to work, and have to base all their knowledge on experiment, observation, and scientific deduction from these methods, provides the main reasons why the aims and goals of medicine have to remain relatively modest, despite some of the remarkable achievements which have been attained.

Finally, it is a normal characteristic of the human body that it wears out. We all know this, and express it in such remarks as 'we all have to die some time'.* What actually happens is that the human body gradually passes its peak in general vitality, capacity for repair, and reproductive power, and in many ways has already passed this peak by the age of thirty or thirty-five. It cannot be renewed once it has reached maturity, and it is clearly not constructed to last an indefinite time.

However, there is yet another way in which there is an echo of that seemingly inescapable element of chaos and

* See Kurt Vonnegut, *Slaughterhouse 5*, Jonathan Cape, London, 1970, p. 3 and *passim*.

disaster with which we were concerned in Chapter One. This is in life's condemnation, by its basic design and process of survival, to prey upon life. Living creatures have to destroy one another in order to go on living, in all except certain categories of vegetable matter, including plants, trees, grass and flowers of the world. Such plants, by gaining their sustenance and developing their structure as well as managing their reproduction entirely by using the sun's energy to synthesize their living matter out of inert mineral elements of the earth's surface, show that life can be created out of energy and elementary lifeless matter. It is not impossible to imagine, or even to design, ways in which this process could have been the basis of much more complicated forms of life, including animal life.

Yet even plants themselves have not a long way to look back in their evolutionary past or forward into their evolutionary future, to betray the sickening and all too familiar process of life preying on life for survival. The simplest forms of vegetable life are the viruses and the bacteria, and we have already taken a brief but sufficiently appalled look at them and what they do. Advancing upwards in the scale of evolutionary complication, we find plants which have evolved sufficiently far to be not simply cross-fertilized by the attentions of the insects, which they attract with their scent and then endow with their germinal pollen; but even to have achieved this status of predators themselves. The sticky-tongued fly-eating plants of the South American jungles will do as a single if spectacular example.

But what should we think of a manufacturing programme designed to produce durable goods, like motorcars and aeroplanes, which could only function and be maintained by a continuous diet of smaller or less powerful articles such as transistor radios, cameras, electric irons, or razors. Yet that is our condition. We may say we did not choose it, but we are none the less bound by it. How do we deal with this in our own hearts, which seemingly yearn to give praise to the great designer of us all?

Some of us simply deny the implications of what we see around us; others even refuse to see it. Freud pointed out the facility of this mechanism as well as its futility: he recognized, in the undisguised antipathy and aversion which people so often feel towards strangers, and particularly identifiable strangers in their midst, a fundamental expression of the infant's exclusive self-love and his consequently helpless explosive aggression towards anything or anyone possessing competitively separate existence. In this respect the infant, as a child, is not only father to the man, but often biologically considerably wiser. For when a man learns or discovers within himself pity and altruism, he has surrendered hostages not simply to fortune, but to logic and reason.

So once again we are slung unceremoniously back upon the ant-heap of life and nature; the predicament as well as the mystery of life itself. For us, perhaps, the human predicament always remains the most crucial and the most poignant of all, if only because we see it so clearly and so well. It is the predicament alike of the individual and of society: to be capable of perceiving what is ideal, and yet achieving only what limitations of instinct, opportunity, and human vulnerability will permit; of conceiving what is good and yet achieving less and less of what is conducive to good. To aim high, but to fall short, to die without having reached one's goal, these are all aspects of our human state. And yet in our human state, they are perhaps all we can expect. Yet, tragically and superbly defiant, we insist to the end on expecting more. Whether our expectations include eternal life, or simply more satisfaction or relief in this one, whether we work, pray, or look to sex,* drugs,† or violence‡ for a release from despair, we are driven alike by some silent merciless necessity. The Greeks knew necessity: to them it was at once the beginning and the end of all human striving and argument. Only the Gods could override necessity; sometimes not even them. Like them it was pitiless, unpredictable, omnipotent.

We have met this necessity before. Indeed its shadow, like a drawn sword, lies across our path constantly in these explorations, and as constantly confronts us. Many years ago, twenty-one to be precise, I thought I had at least a glimmer of an answer to this question. It was embodied in a number of poems, of which that quoted at the end of Chapter One on pages 21–2 was the opening. The collection as a whole was called 'The Way to the Battle', which was also the title of the longest and most important poem. At the end of the collection, there was an essay which formed an appendix to the poem and which was derived from notes originally written during one of the several revisions of the manuscript of the poem itself. At the time, these were a technical device designed to clarify certain emerging ideas, but not primarily intended for publication. When they had served this purpose, they ceased to be essential to the poem: but by then the essay contained in them had acquired an independent existence and so was included.

* See Appendix Three, page 155. † See Appendix Four, page 160.
‡ See Appendix One, page 141.

BUT HOW, IN WHAT?

I want to go back to that essay in time and space to conclude this chapter, turning finally to the poem which twenty-one years ago was the nearest I could get to an answer. In one sense it satisfied me then: it certainly does not satisfy me now. But the stream of thought which I had been seeking to pursue and to follow with you in this chapter would be incomplete without it, and it has its historical place in that stream of thought without which the stream could not have continued.

I had returned in the essay to the theme that there were indeed grounds for believing that there seemed to be some purpose and design underlying the whole of existence; and I acknowledged that for some this belief had the quality of knowledge. I wrote then the passage about 'awareness', which has already appeared on page 24.

This became in the poem 'man's silent merciless necessity to lose himself in God; pour out his scourging fire before an altar that he cannot see . . .'. An altar that, unless he is a mystic or at least an exceptionally gifted man, he will probably never see at all during his lifetime. But for such a man, however base or feeble he may be, there can never ultimately be any doubt of the truth of his awareness, wherever it may lead him, whether or not he dares to follow it or gains the grace to do so –

> This from the first had seemed a challenge
> And from the moment of accepting it
> Each man was circled by his own decision
> Each knew that he had set himself a mark
> To be his triumph or his tragedy.

He is started in fact upon his quest, the perennial quest of mankind – but it is a quest which seems to lead, not to any final goal, but rather to a new beginning, a concept of which he is not even dimly aware when he starts out. It is not as though his journey had no end; that it most certainly has, for if he truly seeks it, or even sometimes if he does not, he is liable suddenly to be confronted by it in the form of spiritual crises in his life which may have very material repercussions as well. At this point he is faced with a critical decision, of whose significance he can never be fully aware, although he is in no doubt of its importance: now he must make the jump.

François Mauriac finds another, equally allegorical way of describing this climax:

> In most men the road of life is a dead end, leading nowhere. But there are some who, even in childhood, realize that they are moving towards an unknown sea. At the very beginning of their journey they are amazed by the bitter violence of the wind and taste the salt upon their lips. On they go until at length, when the last dune has been surmounted, they find themselves in a world of spume and blown sand which seems to speak to them of an infinity of passion. That is the moment when they must choose their path. Either they must take the final plunge, or they must retrace their steps.*

This step which is demanded of the individual can come in a thousand different guises, but in its essence it is an act of faith; symbolized by Mauriac as the final plunge into the unknown sea; by me, as the parachute jump.

'All this leads to the edge of the swaying platform . . .' – to the verge of the unknown sea, to Franz Kafka's Castle, to the coming face to face in one way or another with the ideal of Reality, with the idea of God and the desperate absolute need implanted in every one of us to find him,

* François Mauriac, *The Unknown Sea*, translated by Gerard Hopkins, Eyre & Spottiswoode, London, 1948.

to recognize him in our lives, to love him, and by his grace to live or die for him. And all the time we are stumbling towards this vital stage in our lives: not knowing as yet what it will be, but aware only of our need to reach it, we feel somehow that it will indeed prove to be a climax, 'a final plunge' in Mauriac's words.

'The one step forward, taken or refused, is final. . . .' Yet we are wrong. What we took to be the end is indeed only a beginning. This is one of the ideas running through T. S. Eliot's *Four Quartets*: a similar use of the words 'end' and 'beginning' occurs inescapably in 'The Way to the Battle'. Their use *is* inescapable, because here is one of the fundamental truths of human experience, something which in Eliot's own words:

> . . . has already been discovered
> Once or twice, or several times, by men whom one cannot hope
> To emulate – but there is no competition –
> There is only the fight to recover what has been lost
> And found and lost again and again: and now, under conditions
> That seem unpropitious. But perhaps neither gain nor loss.
> For us, there is only the trying. The rest is not our business.*

'Only the trying': therein lies the artist's single duty. Kafka's way of bringing out this new struggle, which can only begin when the earlier one ends in something deceptively like success, is to open the story of *The Castle* after K., the hero, has made the critical decision. He has already left his own village to seek admission to the Castle and permission to dwell under its protection. He has made his act of faith unreservedly, and even been granted some sort of revelation – a hint that the Castle has use for his

* T. S. Eliot, 'East Coker', *Four Quartets*, Faber & Faber, London, 1944.

special services. The rest of the allegory deals with the next and most testing phase of all – the relentless, unremitting trial of faith and courage which can only begin when man has committed himself deliberately to belief in God, not as an intellectual probability but as the centre and meaning of his life. Then comes 'the long tiring struggle on the ground . . . the lifelong battle . . .' in which success in the accepted material sense may never – perhaps can never – be achieved. It is for this reason more than any other that material success, no matter how honourably gained, well deserved, or apparently innocent, must in this sense always be suspect, and suspect most of all by those who have achieved it.

The poem ends on a note of recognition of the transcendent importance of this final struggle: whatever form it takes, it must constitute for any particular individual the real reason for his existence, just as the earlier search for it constituted the one perennial quest of all mankind, no matter in what aspect it presented itself to him. To have a vocation in life is to have armour in which to fight this battle; to have a vocation for the religious life is perhaps to have the strongest armour of all. But the supremely important thing – the point of the whole poem, and its only justification – is 'the awareness of the open heart, despite the old world and the old distractions', for from this comes the seeking which leads to the swaying platform, to the jump, the terror and the ecstasy, and finally to the acceptance of the lifelong battle, cunning and guile of the old enemy, weakness and hopelessness of separate self.

Without the love of God the whole of this would be meaningless; so indeed would everything else. But such purely negative assertions can never provide positive reasons for belief; nor does the poem attempt to provide them. The function of poetry is essentially interpretive, never purely dialectical. The quest, the crises, and the quest renewed, this time with all the issues sharpened but the final achievement never in man's grasp, yet never finally denied to him . . . this is the theme of the poem.

I
THE WAY TO THE BATTLE

Look upward; Now they come
Men leaping from the dark hatch
Tumbling silently upon the air,
Figures against the sky, bodies caught in the whirlwind
Spun by the slipstream, helpless, tiny,
Buffeted as they fall.

Suddenly the promise is kept
Wonder is made apparent
As in succession the bright canopies open
White veined translucent cupolas with scalloped edge
Whose gathered shroud lines, taut as bowstrings
Tether as seed to thistledown,
Swinging like censers before an altar
Airborne, floating upon the wind
The parachutists. . . .

This, from the first, had seemed a challenge
And from the moment of accepting it
Each man was circled by his own decision
Each knew that he had set himself a mark
To be his triumph or his tragedy
Each in his separate way
Had made his choice:
And to redeem his choice
Must make the jump.

II

I knew there was a world
So far denied me;
A world through which an aircraft
Passed like a shadow at the moment of ascending.
So for an instant was revealed
A mystery as swiftly lost
As it was promised.
Just for that second, as the earth
Streaming beneath our wings, no longer held us
At that tremendous parting from the ground
Almost could we leap from our leaden selves
And burst like singing birds into the sky.

Revelation lies at the heart
Of that split second's parting from the earth.
When the ground that has been racing past,
A flood exulting from a shattered dam,
Suddenly recedes: Ceases to be a torrent
And becomes a pattern.
Then is every detail plain in objectivity.
Then the earth gives up her secrets
As at the last;
Severance is made absolute, the act of parting ends;
Then a man's aeroplane becomes his world
Then, at that critical instant,
Begins his separation.

Once airborne the revealing moment's over
The world within the aircraft now assumes
Earth's own familiar character,
More cramped, more technical, but still a world
Of objects . . . gleaming instruments,
Handles and maps,
A world whose pattern of reality is still unchanged;
Wherein a man can walk,
With something solid underneath his feet;

BUT HOW, IN WHAT?

Wherein dimensions are preserved: gravity's pull
Invests each object with its own stability,
While through transparent panels can be seen
The other world, discrete, beautifully fashioned
A world whose links are weakened, but whose form
Is with man still, in the whole nature of his travelling.

III
There are moments in church
Moments of solemn revelation
When the real presence of God transforms the hearts
Of the people: where He is always
But unacknowledged.
At such moments self is transcended
By the mystery of adoration.
But without abandonment, there can be
No lasting peace on earth or in men's hearts:
Neither a lasting peace nor an enduring conquest
Of self without surrender;
And the moment is past, can be remembered
Will come again, but without abandonment
Is not lifted out of time
Is not eternal. . . .
The passengers gaze out of the aeroplane
Seeing the change from one world to another
They yet remain the same.
Even though sensing the mystery, they may desire it
They are prevented
While they remain confined within the world:
And the moment is past, can be remembered
Will come again, but without abandonment
Is not lifted out of time
Is not eternal.
Easy to blame the aircraft
Because, to those safe in their numbered seats
Within its cabin
Direct experience of mystery remains denied.

THE NEED TO BELIEVE

High on the mountain side,
Edge of the cliff above the distant sea,
Summit of lonely hill, top of tall tower
It has revealed itself. It is all immanence
Demanding all awareness: for it is always there
As it is always here
And always waiting.

But for those who have not sought awareness
Who, though they travel, are not moved;
Are not disturbed by their unquiet hearts
By the silence at the heart of the music
By the shadow of the hours upon their children
By the cry of the wild bird at night . . .
For those the instant's revelation in the aircraft
May be initiation: May be the first
Soft touch moving over the secret strings
Whose final full vibration, still unstirred
Is yet innate in all.

To know the world through which they fly,
Sensed but no longer seen;
Neither the world beneath
Nor yet its closer counterpart within the aircraft
There is indeed a way of penetration
Way of abandonment, of steep decision
An act of faith beyond evasion
A step from which – once made –
No turning back is possible:
There is the jump.

Easy to blame the aircraft
Because – despite its revelation –
Not every passenger is bound to make the jump
Easy to blame the church
Because among all the faithful
Few seem to be saints.

IV
Before the jump is need of preparation
So that decisions made and lessons learned
In calmness and tranquillity shall be remembered
When all else is forgotten;
So that the one step forward
And the response to landing
Build to a pattern, able to prevail
Against the treachery of flinching or of faltering
Against the natural fear and weakness
Against the urge to turn away
From the faint flickering of a far-off light
Because we are afraid that it will blind us;
And we are right, it will.

There is always the physical passion
Agony or ecstasy
In the beginning;
And the climax that comes at the end
Is not the end at all, is the beginning
Of the long battle that on earth is never ending:
Life is short but the war is unending
And of this too there can be no completion
No absolute end or satisfaction in this life.

After orgasm comes the long heaviness of pregnancy
After the tearing agony of bloody birth
Long patient toil of motherhood
The scale always loaded against the challenger
Each battle shadowed by an old defeat
Through each defeat the pattern of one victory.

All this leads to the edge of the swaying platform
To standing poised with the knowledge of the jump before you,
To the long instant that is the end
And the beginning.
The instant that will always be remembered
A sharp clear instant of appalling loneliness,
For this is the jump that you must make alone.

THE NEED TO BELIEVE

Then is fear lost because life is surrendered
No claim remains but to this instant
No courage left but for the one step forward
The step into silence, the surrender
Of all solidity beneath your feet,
The certain fall to death unless
Unless perhaps there is a meaning
Unless what you embrace is true.

You cannot make the jump until you have decided
That you will go whatever be the answer.
Until you have decided
That there is no decision but to go forward.
Until you have faced the end
There can be no beginning.
So when the instant comes all that remains for you
Is the awareness of finality; the readiness.
Until you have jumped there is no more to know.

Sweat-pricked palms and a dry pounding heart
Stiff tongue and silent mouth, the taut strings
Of music and sharp fire that were your nerves,
These are for memory through the ecstasy
They may come after.
These are the terror and the agony
Before extinction of the shuddering flame
That dying is relit: bright burning wind
That tears through temple veils, moves over altars
From east to west blows like a clarion
Yet makes no sound, is yet pure joy
Is here now everywhere and always
Is now and ever shall be
In the beginning, is the end
Is struggling into life, is death, is birth
Is all awakening.

v
Stand in the door
Four words banish all thought from the mind
Except the passive certainty of now
Now is the moment
Now the consummation
And through sudden quietness within the raging storm
Of feeling, small things seen distantly
From the remoteness of that timeless instant
Are distractions, suddenly
Having no power to distract
From a square cottage chimney
Runs a thin plume of smoke
Straight up into the evening sky.
Far away on the ground
A red flare splutters: night's first ghostly gleam
Shines from a curving river. . . .

Go.
   Red light above the door
Changes to green and suddenly you are gone
One step forward and the abyss has opened
Caught in the cloud of the onrushing wind
The unreasonable plunge begins
Meeting of wind and starlight
Parting of spirit and body
No longer schism in the mind, no longer
Self to be known, action decided
No longer sound but the beating of the wind,
No longer sight or the familiar aircraft
Divided by the space in time
In streaming vastness of illumined sky,
Yet out of all falling alone
The empty chaos waiting to be filled
Last note of the muted violin
Slap of the bowstring, flap like an angel's wing
So gathered by a surging might

From the apex of the quivering shroud lines
Leaping from your shoulders
The fall changes into a huge soaring
Like a bright sun the parachute has opened.

Memory of evening sun whose finger shafts
Pierced the long shadows over Carcassonne,
Warm lingered along grey stone turrets
Bathed the vine-laden plains below
In saffron dusk; memory of slow sweeping sails
Of an old windmill slowly turning;
Memory of first circus time in childhood
Tent top and swinging lights, seem to be caught
And filtered through stretched fabric of the canopy.

Heart filled with longing when first sensed
The soft warm touch of suppliant flesh
Struggling with blindly overwhelming strength
To union and to crisis
Divided agony, and agonizing cleavage blotted out
Darkness rent as by a spurting flame
Swallowed by deeper darkness still
And then, for a deceptive transient moment
By peace or sadness:
Heart thus distended or disturbed
Bursting or broken, hungry or for a while assuaged
Is now emptied of all desire
Is now artlessly opened like a flower to sun
Is now absorbed by wonder
Is utterly surrendered, is aware
Of all things save of self, and through all things
Of only one in which are all
Through all of which is one
Now and forever.

Tension and fear and old anxieties
Cease and are stilled
As the old rodent self no longer gnaws
Insatiable upon the wholeness of the spirit

BUT HOW, IN WHAT?

Upon the thread which binds the soul to God.
Yet all the while
The earth swings nearer, and the trees and houses
The railway lines and aerials
Telephone wires and high-tension cables
Bank balances and typewriters
Targets and maps and submachine guns
Ticker tape and confetti and champagne
The box at the opera and the silk tie in the window
Rise up to greet you and enfold you:
For it is the same world, with the old horrors
And the old delights, the terrible beauty
And the treacherous passion, the sodden evil
And the splendid fun.
All the prohibitive complexity of civilization
All the excuses and the stern demands
The whole damning confusion and rationalization
The snickering in the cinema, wringing of hands
In the prison hospital, these and the familiar
Uncountable pressures and presences and distractions
Time killers and time fillers, equally disastrous
Await you as the ground slides suddenly upwards
And you point your feet towards the landfall.
     Then it is over
A sudden jolt and the trained body instantly conforms
Sharp roll like shot rabbit
The long shroud lines curving gracefully to the ground
The canopy no longer taut with air
Expiring quietly in uncomplaining death
Collapse of an angel in the corps de ballet – or perhaps
Tugging with gusty breaths, having to be despatched
By the shrewd pull on the lower shroud lines
On the swift sprint round to the leeward side
Is this then all? Is this immediate elation
This transient exultance, briefly remembered ecstasy
Is this then all, whole heart and fountain of the mystery?

VI

We have been told the jump is but the way
Of getting to the battle;
All that is promised only is fulfilled
In the long tiring struggle on the ground
In the awareness of the open heart
Despite the old world and the old distractions
In the acceptance of the life-long battle
Cunning and guile of the old enemy
Weakness and hopelessness of separate self.

He who has made the jump has progressed only
Enough to find the road that he must follow,
He who has never made it is not lost
For it awaits him;
Nor is he lost who, faced by the jump, has faltered
And been afraid – nor is he lost either
For by humility without despair
Is the way open to him
If he can bear to seek it yet again.

For all there is the jump or the refusal
In one form or another, sooner or later is the coming face to face
For all there is the crisis and the waiting
Not just in time but in eternity
All seeking leads but to the swaying platform
Hearing the secret whisper in the slipstream
And the terror and the ecstasy are there
On the drawing-room carpet as on the side of the mountain
In the bent back of the charwoman
No less than in snow among the crocuses
In swan's flight or the waterfall;
Courage in the quiet answer, the acceptance
Of evil, the acceptance of disaster, no less
Than in the sudden spectacular step forward
The flying plunge, glory of whistling shroudlines
Flap of the opening canopy
The miraculous suspension.

Nothing but love can give the act of faith its value
Nothing but love can give the jump its meaning.
In the instant when there is no separation
God – the Beginning and the End
Is Love.

VII

This would be all – but for the reasonable man:
Who says 'I see no meaning in all this.
I feel no urge to jump out of an aeroplane
Nor do I need to do so
To learn that God is Love
Or rather, that you say that He is Love.
Candidly there is nothing new in that pronouncement
I have seen it on Evangelists' banners
At race meetings; or tracts pushed through my letter box.
It is popular with the Salvation Army
Who march right past my house on Sunday mornings
I have even seen it on a placard
Among the advertisements for shoe polish and lemonade
In the tube station which I use each day;
And quite apart from that –
I don't believe it anyway; for were it true
How could there be wars, or cruelty to children
Or diseases?'
  Eminently reasonable, you will agree
Though not unanswerable.
For we all share his doubt
Or at least act as though we shared it;
All or nearly all of us, each in our numbered seats
Knowing we do not know our destination.
Were we to believe – all or nearly all of us –
To shape our actions to this one belief
We might yet open ourselves to God,
Kingdom of Heaven within our hearts, so be beyond
Wars, cruelty, tyranny of bodies and of selves
So would they cease; As they will never cease

THE NEED TO BELIEVE

In this or that man made Utopia
Even were such a hell on earth attainable.
Easy to answer this: Easy to argue and
Essentially unprofitable: for even argument
Is ultimately but distraction. Love is the only answer.

Nothing but love can give the act of faith its value
Nothing but love can give the jump its meaning.
In the instant when there is no separation
God the Beginning and the End is Love.

3

Who is Jesus Christ, and Why is He?

There is a green hill far away
Without a city wall
Where our dear Lord was crucified
Who died to save us all.

We do not know, we cannot tell,
What pains he had to bear;
But we believe it was for us
He hung and suffered there.*

Those two verses come from a familiar Christian hymn. It was one of the first hymns that I remember hearing in the Methodist chapel to which my parents took me as a child. Its simple but lovely tune, and its equally simple but penetrating words, move me still. There could be other ways of opening this examination of the identity and meaning of the man who claimed that he was the Son of God, shared God the Father's Divinity with him, and was also the Messiah, the Son of Man for whom the Jewish people had waited throughout their history: they wait for him still. So this will be my way.

The theological history of Judaism makes it perfectly clear that the expectation cherished by the Jews was that a

* Mrs Cecil Alexander (1812–95).

man should be born among them who would become their leader and their king. Christ's insistence that his kingdom was not of this world, was not fully accepted by the great majority of his contemporaries who had believed him to be the Messiah; any more than Christ's claim that he was the Messiah has been accepted by orthodox believers of the Jewish faith.

For the first Christians, and indeed for all of us, the facts witnessed and recorded of the life, death, and resurrection of Jesus of Nazareth have to be recognized as crucial. Indeed, the theological position is that they must be accepted as historically true if they are to have the full meaning attributed to them. Moreover, if they are true, the universe in which they could happen must be explained by them; and even if the explanation remains only partial, we can be sure that the final clue is there. No discussion of the world and man's place in it can be adequate that does not take Jesus of Nazareth into account; not simply as a divine eruption into history, mysterious as that must be, but also in one way as a natural and inevitable happening within it. Both the first and the third gospels, by their insertion of genealogies, make this perfectly plain.

> One essential conclusion would seem to be that God's purpose in creation is that His love should awaken the response of love in free human beings, capable of full response to Him in a truly personal relationship. To such a relationship the conventional terms like worship, adoration, and love as we understand them may well be only partly adequate; and perhaps the implication is that what God asks of us is a full expression of creative love in every circumstance in which history may involve us. Among these circumstances all suffering, whether guilty or guiltless, has its place, and in this sense is certainly permitted by God, and can indeed become the

occasion for the outgoing activity of creative love in us, and for the response within us to awaken faith and the creative love of God.

These sentences have a strangely familiar and disturbing ring, as well as a profound impact on me, as I re-read them. They are in fact part of the heritage of an attempt on my part, at one stage in my life, to collaborate with a theologian in an exploration of the meaning and purpose of the central faith of Christianity.* That such meaning and purpose, and such faith, are part of a possible response to man's acknowledged need to believe has already been considered. Seen in this way, the star which the wise men followed, and which hung poised in the sky over the crib in Bethlehem, is the fixed star of hope for all mankind: just as the shadow of the cross and the mystery of the resurrection hang for ever over what might otherwise seem the blindness of our human fate.

There is no escaping these questions in the context of this wholly respectful but sincere inquiry. The answer to them may remain a matter of faith rather than of objectively proven fact; and the search for the implications of both question and answer may lead us to paths we had not thought to encounter. But as perhaps we have begun already to recognize together, the search is inescapable, the questions must be posed, the answers will not and cannot be excluded from our consideration.

As far as anything is certain about the gospels, two

* The quoted paragraph is taken direct from an essay first published by the author in the *St Raphael Quarterly* (New Series, Vol. 2, No. 6), May 1958. This essay was in turn based upon a discussion between Professor L. W. Grenstead and Dr David Stafford-Clark which had, as its immediate purpose and outcome, a memorandum on man's nature and destiny submitted for the consideration of the Archbishop's Commission on Divine Healing.

things emerge again and again with unmistakable clarity. Jesus of Nazareth believed that he was the Christ, Messiah, and the Son of God; and he also believed that part of his task was to reveal by his own divine incarnation an aspect of the loving and merciful God who was his Father. If he was right about these two things, then the answer to the whole mystery and agony of the human predicament is indeed to be found in Christianity. If he was not, Christianity is yet one more beautiful but tragic myth.

In the gospel according to St Matthew, there is a well-known passage concerned with the fate of sparrows and the numbering of all the hairs on all the heads of every human being in the world. This was how Christ sought to convey one aspect of the truth about God, and about man's relationship to God, to his hearers. Man has not always found this relationship either so loving or so merciful. In 1963 I had read a remarkable contemporary novel, *Catch 22*, by Joseph Heller. The basis of the novel is really an examination of man's predicament in the world, and of ways in which men react to this. The hero of the novel is an American airman called Yossarian: an intelligent, sensitive, bitter man, caught up in the savage and frequently ludicrous ways of destruction of the Second World War.

The first quotation is an excerpt from a conversation that he is having with the wife of his dogmatic and insensitive commanding officer. She is a rather silly, unimaginative but basically warm-hearted and generous young woman. They are spending the week-end together.

> 'And don't tell me God works in mysterious ways,' Yossarian continued, hurtling on over her objection. 'There's nothing so mysterious about it. He's not working at all. He's playing. Or else he's forgotten all about us. That's the kind of God you people talk

about – a country bumpkin, a clumsy, bungling, brainless, conceited, uncouth hayseed. Good God, how much reverence can you have for a Supreme Being who finds it necessary to include such phenomena as phlegm and tooth decay in His divine system of creation? What in the world was running through that warped, evil, scatalogical mind of His when He robbed old people of the power to control their bowel movements? Why in the world did he ever create pain?'

'Pain?' Lieutenant Scheisskopf's wife pounced upon the word victoriously. 'Pain is a useful symptom. Pain is a warning to us of bodily dangers.'

'And who created the dangers?' Yossarian demanded. He laughed caustically. 'Oh, He was really being charitable to us when He gave us pain! Why couldn't he have used a doorbell instead to notify us, or one of his celestial choirs? Or a system of blue and red neon tubes right in the middle of each person's forehead. Any jukebox manufacturer worth his salt could have done that. Why couldn't He?'

'People would certainly look silly walking around with red neon tubes in the middle of their foreheads.'

'They certainly look beautiful now writhing in agony or stupefied with morphine, don't they? What a colossal, immortal blunderer! When you consider the opportunity and power he had to really do a job, and then look at the stupid, ugly little mess he made of it instead, his sheer incompetence is almost staggering. It's obvious he never met a payroll. Why, no self-respecting businessman would hire a bungler like Him as even a shipping clerk!'

Lieutenant Scheisskopf's wife had turned ashen in disbelief and was ogling him with alarm. 'You'd better not talk that way about Him, honey,' she warned him reprovingly in a low and hostile voice. 'He might punish you.'

'Isn't He punishing me enough?' Yossarian snorted resentfully. 'You know we mustn't let Him get away with it. Oh, no, we certainly mustn't let Him get away scot free from all the sorrow He's caused us. Someday I'm going to make Him pay. I know when. On the Judgement Day. Yes, that's the day I'll be close enough to reach out and grab that little yokel by His neck and –'

'Stop it! Stop it!' Lieutenant Scheisskopf's wife screamed suddenly and began beating him ineffectually about the head with both fists. 'Stop it!'

Yossarian ducked behind his arm for protection while she slammed away at him in feminine fury for a few seconds, and then he caught her determinedly by the wrists and forced her gently back down on the bed. 'What the hell are you getting so upset about?' he asked her bewilderedly in a tone of contrite amusement. 'I thought you didn't believe in God.'

'I don't,' she sobbed, bursting violently into tears. 'But the God I don't believe in is a good God, a just God, a merciful God. He's not the mean and stupid God you make Him out to be.'

Yossarian laughed and turned her arms loose. 'Let's have a little more religious freedom between us,' he proposed obligingly. 'You don't believe in the God you want to, and I won't believe in the God I want to. Is that a deal?'

The second quotation is simply the last words of a simple father to his fatally wounded son, who is dying in hospital. In fact the son is already dead, and the bandaged figure in the bed is Yossarian himself, pressed into substituting for the original victim because he happens to be a patient himself, and the hospital authorities have got into one of their characteristic muddles. He lies motionless and silent while the boy's father speaks.

The father continued slowly with his head lowered. 'When you talk to the man upstairs,' he said, 'I want you to tell Him something for me. Tell Him it ain't right for people to die when they're young. I mean it. Tell Him if they got to die at all, they got to die when they're old. I want you tell Him that. I don't think he knows it ain't right, because He's supposed to be good and it's been going on for a long, long time, Okay?'

The third quotation is an account of the squadron chaplain's anguished doubts: he had become increasingly miserable and tormented, and,

... was ready now to capitulate to despair entirely but was restrained by the memory of his wife, whom he loved and missed so pathetically with such sensual and exalted ardor, and by the lifelong trust he had placed in the wisdom and justice of an immortal, omnipotent, omniscient, humane, universal, anthropomorphic, English-speaking, Anglo-Saxon, pro-American God, which had begun to waver. So many things were testing his faith. There was the Bible, of course, but the Bible was a book, and so were *Bleak House, Treasure Island, Ethan Frome* and *The Last of the Mohicans*. Did it indeed seem probable, as he had once overheard Dunbar ask, that the answers to the riddles of creation would be supplied by people too ignorant to understand the mechanics of rainfall? Had Almighty God, in all His infinite wisdom, really been afraid that men six thousand years ago would succeed in building a tower to heaven? Where the devil was heaven? Was it up? Down? There was no up or down in a finite but expanding universe in which even the vast, burning, dazzling, majestic sun was in a state of progressive decay that would eventually destroy the earth too. There were no miracles; prayers went unanswered, and misfortune tramped with equal brutality on the virtuous and the corrupt; ...

The final quotation comes from one of the culminating chapters in the book, when Yossarian experiences a nightmare awareness of the cumulative suffering and anguish of the world while he is wandering, absent without leave, through war-time Rome, trying to make up his mind what to do, and surrounded on all sides by the pitiless horror of man's blind, helpless inhumanity to man, and God's apparent indifference to it all.

Almost on cue, a nursing mother padded past holding an infant in black rags, and Yossarian wanted to smash her too, because she reminded him of the barefoot boy in the thin shirt and thin, tattered trousers, and of all the shivering, stupefying misery in a world that never yet had provided enough heat and food and justice for all but an ingenious and unscrupulous handful. What a lousy earth! He wondered how many people were destitute that same night even in his own prosperous country, how many homes were shanties, how many husbands were drunk and wives socked and how many children were bullied, abused, or abandoned. How many families hungered for food they could not afford to buy? How many hearts were broken? How many suicides would take place that same night . . .?

Yossarian quickened his pace to get away, almost ran. The night was filled with horrors, and he thought he knew how Christ must have felt as he walked through the world, like a psychiatrist through a world full of nuts, like a victim through a prison full of thieves. What a welcome sight a leper must have been!

Two sparrows sold for a farthing. In another part of the New Testament the number is five. Each one of them precious, but presumably infinitely less valuable in God's sight than a man. Considered on the same scale a malaria parasite is equally obviously worth considerably less than a sparrow; but they outnumbered sparrows in Christ's lifetime in the world, and they would outnumber them even more completely today but for the efforts of the World Health Organization. There is little room for doubt about the wonder, and the beauty, and the inspiration of life; as we have already seen, there is equally no room for doubt that, as Yossarian pointed out, the way life has been organized is, to say the least of it, surprising even to the mind of man as a designer. For a supernatural design it seems frankly incredible. This is perhaps what has made the idea of God in the Old Testament seem such a cruel, spiteful, vengeful, jealous person, who periodically lost his temper and had constantly to be praised or cajoled or in some way or another prevented from venting his wrath, his senseless abysmal wrath, upon human beings. It is also perhaps why our explorations in the first two chapters have seemed to point so far away from love and so desperately close to chaos; or at best to an exultant, inexplicable splurge of blind creation.

But if Christ was who he said he was, then he was certainly in the best position in history to explain something of the true nature and purpose of God to mankind; and this in turn was part of his own explicit task. If he was what he said he was, then his life has to be scrutinized in whatever detail can be discovered, for the evidence of how a loving God made man would behave towards his fellow men. We need not stumble over tiny crevices and anomalies. Cursing the fig tree which promptly withered could well be an apocryphal story. But what must strike the reader over and over again in his examination of Jesus of Nazareth throughout the story told in the Gospels, is how this man did illuminate the power and impact of love and how perhaps he exemplified it in action – for example, in what are called the healing miracles.

I sincerely believe that a great deal of confusion has been created on the topic of the healing miracles, and I want to consider them in this aspect in a moment. But at this point it can and should be said that no doctor needs to boggle at the concept of the healing miracles, still less at the fact that, if they were possible for Christ, it was only natural that he should use this supernatural power whenever he could. What may be surprising is that it was used on such a limited scale, and sometimes in such archaic ways. The casting out of devils, for example, reminds us that Christ was not only the essence of the reality of God, if his claim must be believed, but that he was also essentially a man of his time. At a conscious level he clearly knew less about malaria and schizophrenia than we know now; and indeed at that level all the discoveries that were yet to be made by the human race after his time must surely have been beyond his human comprehension.

The conflict which must still concern us remains the general conflict between the beauty, inspiration, and love which we see running through life on the one hand; and the waste, cruelty, and helpless destructiveness which we cannot avoid seeing in cold clarity on the other. In the story of Jesus of Nazareth, the crux of this conflict is between the love exemplified by Christ in the New Testament and the arrogance and cruelty of the Old Testament God; and even apparently of the God to whom Christ prayed, and about whom Christ taught. The death of Christ, one of the cruellest deaths at that time devised by man, lasting for over six hours and occurring as a cumulative climax of pain, thirst, exhaustion, and surgical shock, is often referred to as the atonement. The concept of atonement is part of the concept of Judaism; but it did not have, and does not have, the same significance as the human sacrifice of a God made man and a man made God. Bound up with the question of who Christ was is why it all happened as it did. And when we begin to stand back from this and attempt to contemplate it not simply as a historical fact or legend but also as the most significant single event in history (if it was a fact), then we see that the essential precondition for the origin of Christianity as a belief was not necessarily the birth, life, and death of Christ at all.

The essential precondition was that at some point in its history, and for some extraordinary reason, at least a part of the human race had begun to take upon itself the notion that it was responsible for all the evil, waste, and cruelty in the world: that it somehow bore an infinite guilt, which only an infinite and supernatural act of atonement could expiate and assuage. The essence of the Christian position about this is expressed in some of 'the comfortable words' taken from the Communion Service in the Book of Common Prayer.

> Hear what comfortable words our Saviour Christ saith unto all that truly turn to him.
>> 'Come unto me all that travail and are heavy laden, and I will refresh you.'
>> St Matthew, 11, verse 28.
>> 'So God loved the world, that he gave his only-begotten Son, to the end that all that believe in him should not perish, but have everlasting life.'
>> St John, 3, verse 16.
>
> Hear also what Saint Paul saith:
>> 'This is a true saying and worthy of all men to be received, That Christ Jesus came into the world to save sinners.'
>> 1 Timothy, 1, verse 15.
>
> Hear also what Saint John saith:
>> 'If any man sin we have an Advocate with the Father, Jesus Christ the righteous; and he is the propitiation for our sins.'
>> 1 St John, 2, verse 1.

But this proposition can be completely reversed, and can still seem to be valid. Throughout history men have looked at the concept of the loving fatherhood of God and the sacrifice of Christ and have asked 'Why?' Joseph Heller was asking this through the story of Yossarian and his friends and enemies in *Catch 22*. Heller's contemporary indictments do not differ in essence from those which have been made since time immemorial. Moreover, they need making, because unless we face their implications there is no hope of any of us coming to terms with the reality of what we really mean by God, Christ, or love. Without them we can't come to terms with the reality of what we see and experience in the world.

These indictments, these agonized challenges, are inescapable. Voltaire, who had remarked that if God did not exist it would be necessary to invent him, nevertheless wrote his most brilliant contribution in terms of a universe in which purpose and love and mercy could not finally be discovered. Bernard Shaw, in *The Adventures of the Black Girl in her Search for God*, made successive Old Testament Gods appear, each one seeking to impress her; each one being humiliated in turn by her simple common sense. Fyodor Dostoyevsky, epileptic, profoundly religious, and one of the greatest novelists who ever lived, wrote perhaps his greatest novel of all, *The Brothers Karamazov*, when he was over seventy.* In it there occurs the famous passage when Ivan Karamazov tells his saintly brother Alyosha that he is returning God's ticket to eternal bliss. It isn't, says Ivan, that he doesn't believe in God, but when he hears a single child scream in agony until it dies, then he himself wants no part of the mercy of a God that can permit that to happen. If the child can't have that mercy, then he doesn't want it, and so he is returning the ticket.

Probably Dostoyevsky himself had been treated in the primitive custodial-type hospitals of his day, where comparatively few of the patients gained benefit from the

---

* 'Rosewater . . . said that everything there was to know about life was in *The Brothers Karamazov*, by Fyodor Dostoyevsky. "But that is not *enough* any more," said Rosewater' – Vonnegut, *Slaughterhouse 5*.

baffled doctors: and many died with the disorders for which they had been admitted. His epilepsy was life-long, but it did not impair his intelligence and his creative capacity. But the process of which it was a part might well have done. If it had we should never have read his work: never have had it to read. But when he was in those primitive hospitals he might well have heard children there with cerebro-spinal meningitis uttering the heart-rending, teeth-grinding cries which usher them out of the world. That could have been the basis of Ivan's famous renunciation of God's mercy.

During his last hour upon the cross before he died, Jesus himself seems to have come close to a comparable despair of that mercy. This could be one explanation, not often faced, of his heart-rending, mysterious, tragic and yet perhaps transcendent cry, 'Eloi, Eloi, lama sabachthani' – 'My God, My God, why hast thou forsaken me?' This may well represent the extremity of his physical suffering, the extremity of human despair and agony; the extremity indeed of endurable experience at the human level. To the doctor, one implication can be that such an entry into the last extremity that the human organism can endure is itself one of the main revelations of the incarnation, telling us that God both knows and understands our own suffering to the very limit, and that he entered into this so that we should know that he knew, and would know that he could understand.

It could be that he also wanted us to know that considerations of human existence and material well-being in time and space as we know them were not in any way ultimately the final or highest criteria of being.

What a way to teach us: moreover he died, without

being able finally and conclusively to make it clear. After the resurrection Jesus seems not to speak of those last six hours, of what they meant to him; of what he had learned, or of what God in his love wanted us to have learned. Sometimes it seems as though it was the Father who sent him, rather than his fellow men, who stood in need of redemption. Terrible as was the death on the cross, men were later to die even more terrible and tortured deaths under the Inquisition,* and even up to our own day and age in the concentration camps, as the outcome of the horrors we have learned to inflict upon each other. The love, the example, and the death of Jesus have not been able to spare us that.

Perhaps the only redemption which can ultimately be imagined for God at the hands of man, reversing the usual judgement situation, in which man is supposed to receive his judgement at the hands of God, is one in which God is acquitted of indifference or irresponsibility towards the human predicament by the very fact that he himself came down to be one of us.

The central idea of Christianity is that of a God who freely chose to live on our terms and amongst us in that one syllable of recorded time of which the Gospels tell; and who embodied in his life the principle that love between living creatures always was, and always will be, the supreme factor which gives the universe its value. Having repeatedly announced and exemplified this fact in his own life, the man made God and God made man finally suffered death by torture; but even then only after scorn and ridicule had been heaped upon him, simply because he remained true to the ideal of love throughout his life. But

* See Appendix Two, page 150.

if it was necessary for God to become man, and die man's cruellest death, in order to prove not only his love for man but also the necessity of man's love for him and for other men, then we are bound to ask what is the nature of this human predicament which demands so terrible a gesture to enable man to forgive God for creating him in a form inseparable from suffering?

I am not a priest. I cannot speak with a priest's authority, but how might a priest answer Yossarian, or Ivan Karamazov, or even me? Perhaps the first answer he could make would be that we spokesmen for man tend to display a certain arrogance and self-centred bitterness ourselves. We might point out that while Yossarian's criticism, Ivan's 'returning the ticket', and my own suggestion that man has much to forgive God, whatever God may have to forgive man, are all points of view which command sympathy and spring from honest anger; there is still an alternative to them. And, like the Kingdom of Heaven, that alternative must start within the heart of the critic himself.

Of course we should be indignant, morally upset, when we see evil things being done, and done repeatedly. But if our reaction to them is simply to become bitter and evil ourselves, we too will have repeated, not resolved or prevented, the spread of evil. And it is our own ultimate self-centred certainty that makes us arrogant and makes us bitter. The only thing wrong with Ivan Karamazov was his belief that the world as he saw it must be totally explicable by himself; and when it did not agree with what he thought it should be, he turned against it and its creator, if it had one. So with Yossarian, so also with what I have said in this chapter. An answer is to be found in one of

Christ's own statements about the condition for knowing and truly loving God. He said we must learn to love others as ourselves. Whenever we can come anywhere near to doing that, we begin to find some release from indignation, from bitterness, and from anger. We have yielded up that last, all-important thing, the right to put ourselves and our own criticism first. That was the one thing that Ivan Karamazov could not yield up, and so he could never get the answer.

Yet this of course was also exactly what Christ did himself. He yielded up his natural self-concern, his agony in the garden, even finally and deliberately his human and personal existence. Moreover, he did it within the terms and conditions of human suffering in all its desperate reality. He has always lived within the terms of human existence, himself seeming often to insist upon the physical realities of that existence even in his own approach to the healing miracles. When he healed a blind man he did not just stand back and tell the man that he could see; he made a kind of clay from spittle and sand and placed it upon the man's closed eyes. When surrounded by a hungry and tired multitude, he did not simply remove their hunger by an act of grace or faith; he multiplied the means, the ordinary loaves and fishes from a boy's picnic basket, by which their hunger might be naturally satisfied. When he awakened the daughter of Jairus from a coma, he commanded her parents to give her something to eat.

As a doctor I have come to see this as a more natural approach to the healing miracles than the superstitious awe with which they are all too often greeted. The most remarkable thing about the miracles is simply that they represented feats which at that time, and to a lesser extent now, were impossible for mankind at the natural level of existence. But doctors do not find anything particularly remarkable about the ability of Christ to heal: many aspects of healing are still outside their present knowledge, and remain to this extent miraculous.

Napoleon's surgeon-general, Ambroise Paré, tramping round the sickening carnage after a battle in the company of the emperor himself, was rewarded by Napoleon's offering him thanks for healing so many of his soldiers. There are many versions of the surgeon's reply: but the most succinct is, 'I tended them, God healed them.' He was simply reminding the emperor of a natural fact. No one has yet been able to bring back life to a dead human being, although even in the last decade we have learned a great deal more than we knew before about the stages by which death is reached, and when people are 'really dead' or not. But given the power to raise the dead, it is not surprising that Christ should have done it. Every humane doctor would like to be able to do it, every humane doctor who was allowed, say, only six raisings in a professional lifetime, would, like his contemporary colleagues who have to make decisions about who shall and who shall not receive renal dialysis, be far more exercised in his choice of who should receive this miraculous dispensation, rather than whether or not he should exercise it.

Christ healed cases of leprosy. Any one of us would heal them all in an instant, if we could. But there were at least as many lepers suffering and continuing to suffer in Palestine, and indeed throughout Europe, after Christ's death as before his birth.

> The evidence in the New Testament can therefore be taken as showing that the actions of Jesus in dealing with sickness were

human actions wrought in and by His human nature, but with this difference: that His was the one human nature in which the full love of God met its effective response and was completely conveyed to others. This in turn reveals the qualities and powers inherent in human nature when God's love is permitted to work out its full purpose through man.*

Here again I recall the touch of the theologian; it is his argument that I have been expounding in the last paragraph, and I used it deliberately, because it has a ring of certainty and authority which I myself would lack. I am bound therefore to question it, while acknowledging its source.

My own instinctive sympathies are less conforming: closer to those of the desperate challenger, the rebel, like Captain Ahab in *Moby Dick*. Captain Ahab pursues that fearful and symbolic creature, the white whale, throughout the book, with all its marvellous divagations and asides. His crew become increasingly alarmed by this pursuit because they come increasingly to know, so marvellous is the development of this story, that there is something numinous and terrible about Ahab's implacable search for revenge or possibly confrontation and expiation. Whether the white whale stands for God, or for the evil in the world, or for the destructive power of nature, Ahab is determined to get even. Almost at the last, he turns for comfort for a moment to his first mate, Starbuck:

> But Ahab's glance was averted; like a blighted fruit tree he shook, and cast his last cindered apple to the soil.
> 'What is it, what nameless, inscrutable, unearthly thing is it; what cozening, hidden lord and master, and cruel, remorseless

---

* See reference, page 67.

emperor commands me; that against all natural lovings and longings, I so keep pushing, and crowding, and jamming myself on all the time; recklessly making me ready to do what in my own proper, natural heart, I durst not so much as dare? Is Ahab, Ahab? Is it I, God, or who, that lifts this arm? But if the great sun move not of himself; but is as an errand-boy in heaven; nor one single star can revolve, but by some invisible power; how then can this one small heart beat; this one small brain think thoughts; unless God does that beating, does that thinking, does that living, and not I. By Heaven, man, we are turned round and round in this world, like yonder windlass, and Fate is the handspike. And all the time, lo! that smiling sky, and this unsounded sea! Look! see yon Albicore! who put it into him to chase and fang that flying-fish? Where do murderers go, man! Who's to doom, when the judge himself is dragged to the bar?'

Who indeed? And the answer might well be, 'All of us, every single one of us, every man jack of us, we are all doomed the day we are born. . . . Life itself is a fatal illness, an incurable disease.'

Is that such a terrible or an unsayable thing?

Terrible it may be, unsayable it certainly is not. Indeed, it has been said not once but many times, in different ways, by desperately sincere men. Listen to the words of the conquistador, Pizarro, speaking to Atahuallpa, King of the Incas of Peru, and now his captive. Atahuallpa is thirty-three; just about Christ's age when he died. Atahuallpa is soon to die himself, sacrificed with his kingdom to the greed of imperial Spain in the name of Christ. Pizarro, who has conquered his kingdom of over twenty million people with 167 soldiers and knows that the treachery by which this victory was gained is shortly going to be exceeded by the even greater treachery of Atahuallpa's murder, is wracked with the pain of his own old wounds.

83

He is thirty years older than Atahuallpa, who trusts him and is trying to comfort him. Pizarro speaks:

> 'Leave it now. There's no cure or more easing for it. Death's entered the house you see. It's half down already, like an old barn. What can you know about that? Youth's in you like a spring of blood, to spurt for ever. Your skin is singing: "I will never get old." But you will. Time is stalking you, as I did. That gold flesh will cold and blacken. Your eyes will curdle, those wet living eyes. . . . They'll make a mummy of your body – I know the custom – and wrap you in robes of vicuna wool, and carry you through all your Empire down to Cuzco. And then they'll fold you in two and sit you on a chair in darkness. . . . Atahuallpa, I'm going to die! And the thought of that dark has for years rotted everything for me, all simple joy in life. All through old age, which is so much longer and more terrible than anything in youth, I've watched the circles of nature with hatred. The leaves pop out, the leaves fall. Every year it's piglet time, calving time, time for children in a gush of blood and water. Women dote on this. A birth, any birth, fills them with love. They clap with love, and my soul shrugs. Round and round is all I see; an endless sky of birds, flying and ripping and nursing their young to fly and rip and nurse their young – for what? Listen boy. That prison the Priest calls Sin Original, I know as Time.* And seen in time everything is trivial. Pain. Good. God is trivial in that seeing. Trapped in this cage we cry out "There's a gaoler; there must be. At the last, last of lasts he will let us out. He will! He will!" . . . But, oh my boy, no one will come for all our crying.'†

Pizarro has said the unsayable thing. Soon after this he is forced to the final betrayal; he hands his captive King Atahuallpa over to the Spanish soldiers to be strangled as a pagan and a heretic. The religion in whose name these

---

* See Appendix Five, page 165.
† Peter Shaffer, *The Royal Hunt of the Sun*, a play in two acts, Hamish Hamilton, London, 1964.

acts were undertaken had long ceased to bear much resemblance to Christianity as its founder proposed it, or as we might like to think of it today. It was a cruel, remorseless, imperious creed as spread by the conquistadores, and wherever it went it took death with it. Before his death, the king bows to the idea of Christ, because he knows that if he does not, he will be burned, and there will be no body for his father the Sun God to resurrect. He believes in the resurrection and the life as sincerely as Jesus did: Pizarro, who has no time for Christianity, secretly believes and hopes that Atahuallpa is right, and that his corpse will be revived when the first rays of the sun touch it the following morning.

So Pizarro waits for the sun to bring the king back to life as Atahuallpa had believed it would; and suddenly, when the dawn comes up and all the priests with their ancient Peruvian gold masks are bowed in prayer, chanting over the dead naked body of the king as it lies in the centre of the stage, the full power of the sun comes on it and it does not move. Disturbed, frightened, bewildered, and finally in despair they disperse. The king was not in fact immortal. He will not rise again. Pizarro suddenly strikes the body of the dead king and it rolls over on the stage.

'Cheat! You've cheated me! Cheat. . . .
[*For a moment his old body is racked with sobs; then, surprised, he feels tears on his cheek. He examines them. The sunlight brightens on his head.*]
What's this? What is it? In all your life you never made one of these, I know, and I not till this minute. Look. [*He kneels to show the dead Inca.*] Ah, no. You have no eyes for me now, Atahuallpa: they are dusty balls of amber I can tap on. You have no peace for me Atahuallpa: the birds still scream in your forest. You have no joy

for me, Atahuallpa, my boy: the only joy is in death. I lived between two hates: I die between two darks: blind eyes and a blind sky. And yet you saw once. The sky sees nothing, but you saw. Is there comfort there? The sky knows no feeling, but we know them, that's sure. Martin's hope, and de Soto's honour, and your trust – your trust which hunted me: We alone make these. That's some marvel, yes, some marvel. . . .'*

The marvel for Pizarro is to discover how deeply he has been moved; but even so his dream has been shattered: just as the dream of Christianity would have been strangled at birth if Christ had not risen from the dead. Pizarro is lost, because of that shattering; and because he personally never had any faith in the Christ for whom he went so brutally to war.

The legend for Atahuallpa and for Christ was the same: the expectations of their followers and believers were the same: only the end, as history records it, is different.

Has that difference changed the world for all time? And what is all time, what is this eternity of heavenly bliss to which Christ directed our thoughts, and where God our Father supposedly awaits us? Is it indeed conceivable to us, and are we, as Karl Barth said, 'the creature between heaven and earth'? If we are Christians, we have to believe all of that. Can we? Do we?

* Peter Shaffer, op. cit.

4

IF THERE BE NO GOD

How Then can I be a Captain?

So far the aim of this work has been to confront a certain desperate havoc which follows upon our daring to ask the questions which inevitably confront us when we recognize some of the inescapable contradictions between religion and life. It might seem that, like a victorious army which has overrun itself, our forays into a search for the meaning behind these contradictions have over-stretched our lines of communication, and left us nothing but devastation in our wake. An army in this position must pause to re-group. It is time we did the same.

One of the patients I have seen whom I will never forget was an accountant in his early forties. Three years before I was asked to see him, his brain had begun to degenerate for reasons which are still not fully understood by our profession. We only know that this happens to a small but definite proportion of the population. The actual brain cells begin to die long before their time, and are replaced by scar tissue, and gradually every vestige of the patient's memory, judgement, attention, concentration, and indeed total personality, recognizable to all who knew him, begin to crumble and disintegrate. Of course, if we believe that the essence, the spirit of man, survives death then we must believe that it also survives the decay of the brain which occurs in pre-senile dementia, which is what this patient had. But it is extremely difficult to accept the evidence presented to us when we see a body that is still living but in which the spirit can apparently no longer find any way of communicating or signalling its presence.

The brain may indeed simply be the instrument whereby we are conscious of our human existence: and if our brain begins to die before we do, we have, to that extent, died even though our body goes on living. But I remember the wife of this man going to see him in the hospital where he lived his last eighteen months, dutifully and desperately visiting the outward appearance of the husband whom she knew and remembered, but who now had no word of recognition for her, consulted a wrist-watch about the time when she should leave, although for him time was meaningless, for he remembered nothing of today or yesterday, looked forward to nothing, registered apparently nothing. This she found unbelievably cruel to accept, even to bear. Unbelievably difficult to equate with the idea of a loving, creative God. And who can blame her? If we return for a moment to the Bible, we are reminded in the Old Testament that God was not always just, merciful, or explicable in the actions or withdrawals attributed to him. Two examples from the Old Testament will suffice.

The first comes from Psalm 89. This is a long psalm, its precise authorship uncertain, but it appears to be written on behalf of King David, to whom God had made a singularly important personal promise. The two critical verses are the thirty-fourth and the thirty-ninth. The thirty-fourth is the reminder of the promise and the thirty-ninth the psalmist's comment on it.

In verses 34-5 God is alleged to have said (Revised Standard Version):

> I will not violate my covenant, or alter the word that went forth from my lips. Once for all I have sworn by my holiness; I will not lie to David.

Verse 39 is then the psalmist's comment on behalf of King David:

> Thou hast renounced the covenant with thy servant; thou hast defiled his crown in the dust.

God here is thus personally and openly accused of betrayal; just as in his last hour his son is recorded as having cried out, demanding to know why he had forsaken him.

The second example is provided by Job. It is the subject of an entire monograph by Jung,* which should be read in its original context. Its gist can be concisely conveyed.

God, allegedly not having a great deal to do at the time, was waylaid by the devil, and personally tempted. 'Look at Job. He's one of your best men of course, but then everything's going well with him. He probably wouldn't think so much of you if everything went wrong with him.' God is incensed, and put upon his mettle. Easily tempted, he falls into temptation and starts to smite Job. First Job's possessions, his herds of goats and cattle, then his wives and children and finally his health, are taken from him in a series of remorseless blows. The devil urges God to go farther. 'You haven't done enough yet, of course he still believes in you, try him further. . . .' God does. Finally Job is reduced to a poverty-stricken, wretched, lonely, sick man, scratching himself with bits of pottery,

---
* C. G. Jung, *Answer to Job*, Routledge & Kegan Paul, London, 1952.

surrounded by erstwhile friends who insist on pointing out that this must all have been his own fault because God is just. Job cannot understand it, but he attempts to maintain his loyalty, and to keep his counsel.

Finally God speaks to Job out of a whirlwind – and what does he say? Nothing whatever about his part in it, about the reasons for it. Not even that he is sorry. He begins by upbraiding Job for expecting any answer, and then says over several chapters what an enormously successful and unique God he is. 'Where were you,' he demands of Job, 'when I laid the foundations of the earth?' Job, still scratching away and cowering in terror, hasn't any answer to that. God's eulogy of himself continues, even exceeding what most of his prophets were able to manage elsewhere in the Old Testament. 'Who made that Leviathan? What part had you in that? . . .' God's triumph is complete. Job humbly acknowledges that it is, and that no doubt he himself was in the wrong somewhere. And God is immediately delighted. He restores Job's health, replaces his herds, and even gives him new wives, and new children, and Job lives until he is over one hundred and forty.

What are we to make of this extraordinary story, with its climax of God providing replacement wives and children for the saintly man whose life he has deliberately wrecked. What human father would go to his son, after murdering that son's family, and expect to restore all the trust and faith of the old relationship by offering the son replacements on this scale: 'Well, cheer up, son, here's your new wife and your new children – they'll do you, won't they?'

Surely the real lesson from this Old Testament story is

that it is an almost flawless example of men trying to make sense of their experience of reality, and their need to believe in a personal God. This God they see as like themselves: and from time to time they are quite unable to get him out of the mess that he seems to have got himself into; even a supernatural person cannot be entirely exculpated from the catastrophes which are part of the entire created world. The malaria parasites, the famines, the earthquakes, the droughts, the tidal waves, the inescapable cruelty and waste – how to get God out of that? Perhaps the Old Testament is, in fact, a revelation of the idea of God translated into human terms by man; and perhaps that translation was attempted with only poetic inspiration and imagination to guide the translators.

If the Old Testament were the last word about God and his love of man, we might still cherish the concept of a God of love; but we could not help concluding that there is in the heart of man a truer answer to the nature and depth of love than is to be found in much of the chronicles of the Old Testament. But then we come to the New Testament, which is something else indeed. If the idea of God in the Old Testament is man's translation of an inconceivably difficult concept into human terms, the fact of Christ in the New Testament may perhaps be man translated by God into divine terms. This is what the New Testament says that God intended. This is what Christ himself said he was. The son of God, the son of man, the incarnation of God. That was his explicit statement. If you are a Christian, that is what you believe. If you are a Christian, you listen to what God said and what Jesus of Nazareth said, and you try to make sense of it. Clearly Christ had a better opinion of God when he spoke about the sparrows and the hairs of the head of everyone in the world being numbered than anyone in the Old Testament could possibly have had. But in the natural world around us, sparrows are falling to the ground all the time; and it is certainly hard to conceive that God spends his time keeping count of them all. Indeed, it is hard to conceive the point of his simply keeping count of the hairs of everybody who had been cut down in one way or another by sickness, cruelty, revenge, disease, war, famine, or torture throughout the history of mankind.

In the Chapter Three we saw how lost and desperate Pizarro was. He was a general, ostensibly fighting for the Church of Christ on Earth. Are we ourselves any the less lost or desperate when we confront our faith?

Cardinal Newman embraced the self-same faith which Pizarro had rejected. Newman uttered its dogma in this breathtaking passage:

> She [the Catholic Church] holds that it were better for sun and moon to drop from heaven, for the earth to fail, and for all the many millions who are upon it to die of starvation in extremest agony, as temporal affliction goes, rather than that one soul, I will not say should be lost, but should commit one single venial sin, should tell one wilful untruth . . . or steal one poor farthing without excuse. . . .*

To how many of us does this represent a literal belief which can influence every action of our day-to-day lives?

'Everything in nature,' wrote George Santayana, 'is lyrical in its ideal essence, tragic in its fate, and comic in its existence.' This supremely penetrating observation on life

* J. H. Newman, *Lectures on Anglican Difficulties*, 1864.

may have taken its foundation from some observations which he had made on the general subject of tragic philosophy. He is here writing about inspiration, and its conflict with truth.

> Inspiration has a more intimate value than truth and one more unmistakably felt by a sensitive critic, since inspiration marks a sort of spring-tide in the life of some particular creature, whereas truth impassively maps the steady merciless stretches of creation at large. Inspiration has a kind of truth of its own, truth to the soul; and this sincerity in intuition, however private and special it might be, would never conflict with the truth of things, if inspiration were content to be innocently free and undogmatic, as in music or lyric poetry. The inmost vegetative impulses of life might then come to perfect flower, feeling and celebrating their own reality without pretending to describe or command reality beyond, or giving any hostages to fortune. But unfortunately animals cannot long imitate the lilies of the field. Where life is adventurous, combative and prophetic, inspiration must be so too. Ideas, however spontaneous, will then claim to be knowledge of ulterior facts, and will be in constant danger of being contradicted by the truth. Experience, from being lyrical, will become tragic; *for what is tragedy but the conflict between inspiration and truth* [author's italics]?*

Faced by these conflicts, these contradictions, what are we to do? Since they are inescapable, one thing that we cannot and must not do is to attempt to deny them in order to preserve our faith. Perhaps we have reached the stage when some kind of affirmation is essential to us; but that affirmation must be rooted in the answers to, or at least a recognition of the validity of, the questions we have discovered. Affirmations themselves are not particularly

---

* Norman Henfrey (ed.), *Selected Critical Writings of George Santayana*, Vol, I, Cambridge University Press, 1968.

difficult to discover. Here is one from the Old Testament (Ecclesiastes 3 : 11):

> He has made everything beautiful in its time; also he has put eternity into man's mind, yet so that he cannot find out what God has done from the beginning to the end.

That is an affirmation no less positive, no less convincingly authoritative, and no less mysterious than George Santayana's. And so, like designers of the latest jet which has crashed on take-off, we are forced back to the drawing-board, haunted by now perhaps by the idea that the price to be paid for understanding is beyond us: we have not been equipped with the resources, and may never find them.

If Jesus paid that price, whose was the bill? and why was it presented? What has our religion to say in the present state of the world? Collectively, we cannot escape the feeling that there must be an answer (just as Pizarro predicted to his listener the compulsive expectation that at the last of lasts the jailer must come to release us from our prison), but perhaps the answer is incomprehensible unless we bear in mind the warning of the physicist, Schrödinger, that an essential precondition of understanding the world is to be able to conceive of it as without one's self.

It is difficult not so much because it is a consciously painful process but rather because it is intrinsically so very hard to imagine the world going on in the absence of one's conscious perception of it: to conceive of all that participation without one's self as a participant. And most of all it is difficult because, at the very essence of our perception of the world and ourselves and everyone else in it, there is the sense of time, which is finally a purely subjective sense: to paraphrase Descartes, we experience time, and therefore it is. If we were not there to experience it, would it and the necessities which it imposes still exist at all?

Part of Schrödinger's challenge to us to approach the problem of imagining the world as it really is by imagining it without ourselves is to prepare the way for a new and revolutionary treatment of time; one that has not become any easier to grasp subjectively, simply because it is now so familiar a part of the mathematical equations of the space–time continuum, in which time is simply one more dimension of measurement. The concept of the space–time continuum is inseparable from modern physics, and modern physics probably approaches closer to the material nature of reality than any other conceptual framework which we possess. Yet this is in itself an abstract concept, just as the concepts of pure mathematics are abstract concepts. To recall the words of Sherrington in quite another context, they are 'without sensual confirmation, and remain without it for ever . . .'.

I have written elsewhere* about the nature of time from the standpoint of a doctor and a neuro-physiologist; and I shall not repeat here what I have written there. Yet, bidden by the very necessity to which Schrödinger draws our attention, we shall have to return in the last chapter to a consideration of time and subjectivity† when we attempt to ponder upon the real meaning of existence, upon the

---

*'Current Theories on Conscience and Consciousness', a discourse to The Royal Institution, Friday, 9 May 1969; also 'Reflections on Time and Consciousness', BBC Third Programme broadcast, Thursday, 18 September 1969.

† See Appendix Five, page 165.

system of rewards, promises, threats, and demands with which all religions confront us, and to the way in which we can accept and interpret them – or, failing totally to interpret them, finally to reject them.

But, for the moment, we may gain an even starker recognition of this necessity to conceive of the world without ourselves if we observe how it looks to honest and forthright men who cannot relinquish an attitude of human judgement towards it in their own approach to the problem. We may take first a largely secular approach – that of General Omar Bradley – who is reported as having said:

> With the monstrous weapon man already has, humanity is in danger of being trapped in this world by its moral adolescence. Our knowledge of science has clearly outstripped our capacity to control it. We have too many men of science: too few men of God. We have grasped the mystery of the atom and rejected the sermon on the mount. Man is stumbling through a spiritual darkness while toying with the secrets of life and death. The world has achieved brilliance without wisdom, power without conscience. Ours is a world of nuclear giants and ethical infants. We know more about war than we know about peace, more about killing than we know about living. This is our twentieth century's claim to distinction and to progress.

Not very different sentiments, but expressed perhaps with more humility and greater penetration, are to be found in one of Rex Warner's prize-winning essays in the book *The Cult of Power*,* first published in 1946. This particular essay is entitled 'May 1945', and the author is recalling the optimism of the early and enthusiastic proponents of the League of Nations in the years which

---

* Rex Warner, *The Cult of Power and other Essays*, John Lane, The Bodley Head, London, 1946.

immediately followed the end of the First World War, the most condensed and convulsive cataclysm of man-made horror which had yet engulfed Europe.

Of course the lecturer and those like him were right in all that they said. Yet how hopelessly inaccurate were his forecasts! How unjustified was his buoyant step! How blind was his trust in legality! He and many meant well and did their best for obvious decency. They proposed and supported what were obviously desirable ends; but they and all their work were swept away like leaves in the coming storm.

At about the same time as we were listening to the lecturer the greatest of our poets may have been writing, or preparing for publication, his poem 'The Second Coming'. He wrote:

> Turning and turning in the widening gyre
> The falcon cannot hear the falconer;
> Things fall apart; the centre cannot hold;
> Mere anarchy is loosed upon the world,
> The blood-dimmed tide is loosed, and everywhere
> The ceremony of innocence is drowned;
> The best lack all conviction, while the worst
> Are full of passionate intensity.

And, in a general dismay, he puts the question:

> And what rough beast, its hour come round at last,
> Slouches towards Bethlehem to be born?

Yeats' analysis of the situation after the First World War has been proved to have been far more accurate, though less encouraging, than any analyses made by lecturers from the League of Nations Union.

Those analyses looked sound enough; they looked like common sense; they are what people are saying today, though with rather less faith and rather less enthusiasm. Yet it was Yeats who was right. Things fell apart, and the falcon could not hear the falconer. Before very long it became clear to almost everyone that the First World

War had settled nothing at all and it gradually became certain that, unless something was done about it quickly, a second world war was inevitable. . . .

The fact that Yeats' pessimism was justified, while all the common sense in the world proved, without ceasing to be common sense, ineffective, is certainly one of the facts which may have a sobering effect upon our celebrations of the present victory. Yet it is a fact that can prove helpful if it confirms our belief that man does not live by common sense alone, and that the wider outlook of the poet not only gives men pleasure but must also play a part as important as that played by any statesman in the regulation of life and even in the establishment of a system of general security.

Unless we recognize that 'the centre cannot hold', no patching of the circumference will help for long. In the centre is still the same frustration, the same isolation, the same falling away from dignity. There are no agreed standards or values which go deeper than the trivialities of common sense, and these trivialities become more and more concerned with personal security and the possession of cash. Moral feelings are invoked in time of war and, with less success, by politicians in peace-time; but these feelings are growing weaker, resting as they do on assumptions which are no longer generally agreed upon. Many, . . . have fought against fascism in the belief that each individual has a unique value and that no state or organization of men should be permitted to override or crush what is each individual's uniqueness, his personality; yet this is a belief which, in the past, has rested on the belief in a God for whom every soul is valuable and, without the belief in God, the strange paradox, so contrary to the trend of events, that the individual is uniquely important, is, to say the least, not easy to justify. . . . Our 'practical' life is superstitious and the main objects of our superstition are 'science' and 'efficiency'. Since the age is superstitious we do not even achieve a life that can be called either scientific or efficient; we merely pay lip-service to what is vaguely understood to be admirable, and are encouraged at every turn to accept the advice of people whom we think of as 'experts'. There is an expert on the atom, an expert on astronomy, an expert on marketing and

HOW THEN CAN I BE A CAPTAIN?

on housing, but there are no experts on how to live, and it seems *that this is a subject in which we are not greatly interested* [author's italics]. . . .*

At the time when he wrote this, Rex Warner would almost certainly have described his own attitude to the central problem of man's belief as one of hopefully constructive agnosticism. Indeed these, as I recall them, were the words he actually used to me about it in a conversation we had at that time.

Later we continued the fruits of one brief war-time meeting in sporadic correspondence, and I have in front of me a letter from him which I kept because of many passages in it which I found extremely illuminating, although I have no record of what I wrote by way of eliciting them. At one point he says:

> I should judge from your letters that you are much more consciously religious than I am. I certainly accept your statement that the wild goose [in his novel *The Wild Goose Chase*] is a religious symbol, but I am still myself uneasily sceptical where religion is concerned. So when religion comes into my books – as it does very largely – it comes almost despite myself. . . .

At the beginning of *The Wild Goose Chase*, which I believe to be one of the most ambitious allegorical novels written in English in the twentieth century, Rex Warner sets this poem, which precedes the opening chapter:

> Wild Goose, I made you a symbol of our Saviour,
> with your fierce indifference to bye-laws and quiet flying,
> your unearthly song, your neck like thunder and lightning,
> and your mysterious barbaric love.

---

* See also Appendix Five, page 165.

> O missionaries and motor-cyclists!
> Let us at daybreak honour the flying host,
> the yelping hounds of air who, with blood for essence,
> thrust like live shells through the speedways of heaven
> above low coasts, over bed of rotting reed.
>
> By light-houses, through showers of ice, listen
> suddenly for onrush of wings, or from the storm
> the bell-like note of an outriding voice.*

From my own point of view, that product of a combination of hopefully constructive agnosticism and uneasy scepticism about religion is far more exciting and, in the most profound sense of the word, optimistic than many far more didactic pronouncements, such as that of General Omar Bradley quoted above.

Nevertheless, it seems to remain the prerogative of the theologians to step firmly from the unknown into the totally unknowable without batting an eyelid. Compare this passage from a recent straight-down-the-line Christian essay published in *The Times* by Dr F. R. Barry, former Bishop of Southwark:

> Obviously, if we do not believe in God there can be nothing further to be said about it. But the burden of guilt in our society may be due in part to secular man's attempt to shoulder his human responsibility in a world which he assumes to be godless, in which there is neither grace nor forgiveness. Moral experience points beyond itself and may prove to be self-contradictory except within the context of Theism.
>
> An objection is often raised against Christianity for deriving its ethics from its theology. What is good or right, it is argued, is good or right independently of any belief in God. So far as it takes one,

---

* Rex Warner, *The Wild Goose Chase*, John Lane, The Bodley Head, London, 1938.

HOW THEN CAN I BE A CAPTAIN?

Christians must agree with that. Things are not good because God 'commands' them.

But, for Christians, God is the supreme goodness, at once eternal perfection and the source of all that is good in the temporal order. It is by perfection that we are 'judged', – 'transcendant' and ever beyond our reach – and in God's sight therefore no man living is justified. All alike fall short of the glory of God. But to recognize that brings tolerance and compassion and is our defence against that self-righteousness by which men and their institutions, including the church, tend to be corrupted. It is God who pronounces the judgement, not man, he alone knows the secret of the heart; and sinful man may not judge his brother. . . .

Let me single out just one part of that passage for further comment. The one which begins, 'But, for Christians, God is supreme goodness', and ends, 'and in God's sight therefore no man living is justified. All alike fall short of the glory of God.' This, in one sense, sums up for me the particular personal hopelessness of getting any basic message from theology. The promises and the conclusion are so inextricably entangled, and so seemingly insightlessly proclaimed, that the entire argument seems like a pyramid inverted and then balanced precariously upon its tip. I can find neither stability nor evidence of final truth in this kind of argument. Not for nothing, indeed, was reasoning along these lines once described with devastating impact by a pure scientist of my acquaintance as 'a pyramiding of unknowns'.

Nevertheless Rex Warner has already indicated that man needs a sense of order, even perhaps of destiny, and that he cannot rest content until he has at least sought it, whether or not he ever finds it. In another essay from the collection already cited,* marvellously entitled

* Rex Warner, *The Cult of Power*.

'Dostoyevsky and the Collapse of Liberalism', he reviews some of the same aspects of the novel *The Brothers Karamazov* as those to which I have already made reference. But he takes his constructive criticism, both of the author and his work, very much farther, considering also its foundations in Dostoyevsky's almost uncanny perceptions about the human nature of human beings, and starting from Ivan's famous assertion that he must 'return the ticket'. Warner covers the whole sweep of the central idea of this religious controversy in a survey of the exchanges between Father Zosima, the spiritual instructor of Alyosha, Ivan's saintly brother, and Ivan himself; in this extract Zosima is speaking, and Warner goes on to balance Zosima's, Alyosha's, and Ivan's powerfully stated articles of faith.

> 'Remember particularly,' he says, 'that you cannot be a judge of anyone. For no one can judge a criminal, until he recognizes that he is just such a criminal as the man standing before him, and that he, perhaps, is more than all men to blame for that crime.' This is a conviction which is constantly recurring in Zosima's discourses, that 'all are responsible for all'. This conviction and the mystical love on which it rests constitute the escape from the horrors of isolation, 'the pride of Satan', and that hell which is 'the suffering of being unable to love'.
>
> So mystical a faith is, of course, beyond the grasp of the atheistic reason, yet we can follow the steps in experience and emotion by which Zosima has reached it. He is fully aware of the intellectual dilemma of the individual reason, and the dangers of the plague 'from the interior of Asia'. He quotes with approval a conversation he had in early life with a friend. 'To transform the world, to re-create it afresh, men must turn into another path psychologically. Until you have become really, in actual fact, a brother to everyone, brotherhood will not come to pass. No sort of scientific teaching, no kind of common interest, will ever teach men to share property and privileges with equal consideration for all. . . . Everywhere in

these days men have, in their mockery, ceased to understand that the true security is to be found in social solidarity rather than in isolated individual effort.'

To Zosima the transformation of the world from 'this terrible individualism' to the solidarity of human brotherhood is inconceivable without 'the sign of the Son of Man', without an acknowledgement of 'the divine mystery in things' which can be reached by love and which can free men from hatred of themselves and others....

This [all-embracing love] is the final answer to the contradictions and cruelties of the analysis of life from the stand-point of the individual intellect; that life is too big to be so approached. 'God took seeds from different worlds and sowed them on this earth, and his garden grew up and everything came up that could come up, but what grows lives and is alive only through the feeling of its contact with other mysterious worlds. If that feeling grows weak and is destroyed in you, the heavenly growth will die away in you. Then you will be indifferent to life, and even grow to hate it.'

And this is indeed the fate which overtakes Ivan, in spite of what he describes as 'this frantic and perhaps unseemly thirst for life in me'. In him the dilemma which we have been attempting to describe is more consciously felt and more clearly expressed than in any other of Dostoyevsky's characters. What makes Ivan more imposing and more sympathetic than the Raskolnikovs and Stavrogins is just this fact that he is uncannily and yet not unnaturally conscious of where he is going, right up to the verge of madness. ... He can understand and, in a part of his nature, he longs for the mystical experience of Zosima, the feeling of 'contact with other mysterious worlds'. But he is, like the devil of his hallucination, 'predestined to deny'. And denial brings no satisfaction. He is poised continually between two views of the universe. Either Zosima's dream is correct, the paean of praise from the whole world to its Creator, the harmony of love and understanding; or else there is no God, and life is conducted in the sphere where 'all things are lawful'....

In his long conversation with Alyosha ... Ivan expresses, with extraordinary force, the intellectual and moral arguments against the 'harmony'. . . . He imagines the suffering of the whole world and, in particular, the torture of wholly innocent children, and he concludes that nothing can ever justify such doings. A chorus of praise from the whole universe may ascend to heaven. Complete and perfect understanding may be reached. The mother of the tortured child may embrace the torturer. Ivan himself and those like him may cry with the rest, 'Thou art just, O Lord!' Yet still the fact remains of children having suffered before this state of universal love is reached, and nothing can justify this one fact. No one has a right to forgive this, and if it cannot be forgiven, 'what becomes of harmony? . . . I would rather be left with my unavenged suffering and my unsatisfied indignation, even if I were wrong. Besides, too high a price is asked for harmony; it's beyond our means to pay so much to enter on it. And so I hasten to give back my entrance ticket, and if I am an honest man I am bound to give it back as soon as possible. And that I am doing. It's not God that I don't accept, Alyosha, only I most respectfully return Him the ticket.'

This, as Alyosha points out, is 'rebellion', and Ivan immediately admits 'one can hardly live in rebellion, and I want to live'. But more urgent than anything is his determination to 'stick to the fact'. Alyosha can only meet the facts that have been so far adduced by assuring his brother that there is a Being who 'can forgive everything, all and for all, because He gave His innocent blood for all and everything'. This is the occasion for Ivan's allegory 'The Grand Inquisitor', in which religion, in the sense in which it is dear to Aloysha and to Zosima, is again attacked from the two standpoints of reason and of 'love of humanity'.

The story of Jesus returning again to earth and being arrested by the Inquisition might seem a likely framework for satire against the hypocrisy of institutionalized religion; but Ivan's allegory is far more profound than that. The Grand Inquisitor is far from being a hypocrite. He is one who, like Ivan, has imagined the beauties of the 'harmony' and, from motives of humanity, has 'returned the ticket'. . . .

The Grand Inquisitor sees in the teaching of Jesus something positively menacing to men's happiness. It does not 'stick to the fact', but enjoys an acceptance of the universe together with a freedom of thought and conscience which are quite beyond man's capacity. What men really desire is to be fed and to have their minds at rest, to be spared the agonies of doubt and decision. . . .

In each temptation Jesus refused to deprive men of freedom, and history in each case, according to the Grand Inquisitor, has proved Him wrong. He might have given them bread and fed them like a flock of sheep. Instead He preferred 'the bread of Heaven' which could in any case only be the sustenance of a small minority. And this is the result: 'Dost Thou know that the ages will pass, and humanity will proclaim by the lips of their sages that there is no crime and therefore no sin; there is only hunger. "Feed men and then ask of them virtue!" – that's what they'll write on the banner which they will raise against Thee.' . . . The old Inquisitor is, like Ivan himself, one who has longed for spiritual perfection, for the harmony of which Zosima speaks. 'But yet all his life he loved humanity, and suddenly his eyes were opened, and he saw that it is no great moral blessedness to attain perfection and freedom, if at the same time one gains the conviction that millions of God's creatures have been created as a mockery, that they will never be capable of using their freedom . . . that it was not for such geese that the great idealist dreamt his dream of harmony. Seeing all that he turned back and joined – the clever people.'

So in Ivan's allegory 'the clever people' are those who have the power to imagine God and yet who, sticking to 'the fact', reject him. The consciousness of their own power and their feeling for humanity lead them to make life tolerable, by efficient organization and by all kinds of lies and deceptions, for the wretched masses of mankind who lack both the strength and the desire for freedom. . . .

Not much reflection is needed to see how apposite to the modern world is this allegory. . . .

Earlier in the same essay Warner has taken an incident from *The Possessed* to pinpoint just that need of order and certainty which I have earlier described as man's 'silent merciless necessity'. He recalls an occasion when, during a discussion among the secret revolutionary band of intellectuals in a cellar in St Petersburg, at which members of the public are somewhat rashly permitted to attend – a kind of open teach-in on atheism – an old-fashioned military man suddenly gets to his feet and exclaims, 'If there is no God, how can I be a captain, then?' Several of the young atheists laugh at the old gentleman, but Stavrogin's comment on the incident is 'he expressed a rather sensible idea'. Stavrogin, despite being the most extreme of them all, is also the most perceptive and intelligent. And indeed the old man did express a perfectly sensible idea.

In one of his best-known sonnets, Shakespeare, in paying tribute to true love, gives it this unforgettable tribute of quality:

> ... Love is not love
> Which alters when it alteration finds,
> Or bends with the remover to remove:
> O, no! it is an ever-fixed mark,
> That looks on tempests and is never shaken;
> It is the star to every wandering bark,
> Whose worth's unknown, although his height be taken.*

The ever-fixed mark, the star, the fixed caring-point in an otherwise apparently uncaring world, that looks on tempests and is never shaken; this is the goal for which, whether we wish to or not, we remain bound to search. We need our fixed points, we must have them if there is to be any order in our assessment of the world, any foundation for status, any authority in hierarchy. With these things, we can envisage law and order; without them, we know we fall blindly into chaos.

* William Shakespeare, *Sonnets*, No. CXVI.

Yet what is the origin of this need to know our own and everyone else's place in the world, and its relationship to some fixed system of values? It is not in fact based on love. It is based on something quite different: the inescapable fact of our own tragic self-centredness. Like all social animals, man carries within the pattern of his nervous system what will emerge as the concept of what has been called the dominance hierarchy. Seen in a lower order of creation, domestic fowls, it is perhaps better known as the pecking-order. Observe any bunch of chickens running free in a chicken-run on a farm, and you will discover that they have among them an established pecking-order. Where there is a rooster among the hens, his sexual value to the rest will give him unquestioned dominance. But even among his many mates, the reality and existence of the pecking-order is most starkly demonstrated. Hen A can peck hen B with impunity; hen B enjoys a similar privilege at the expense of hen C. At the bottom of the pecking order are perhaps hens P and Q, who occasionally peck half-heartedly at each other but dare not peck anyone else. Whenever a new hen is introduced into the collection, its place in the pecking-order will be rapidly established; sometimes high, sometimes low.

It is entirely instinctive and inherent for the new hen to accept whatever place it is accorded. Failure to accept it, for example by pecking hens higher in the pecking order, will sooner or later result in all the established hens turning on it and quite possibly pecking it to death. Social animals, which have to have fixed rules for their co-existence side by side if their conditions are to be tolerable, have these rules built into their nervous system if they are fairly simple; but the higher up the evolutionary tree you study them, the more an element of consciousness and awareness enters into this concept of the dominance hierarchy.

Apes and baboons appear to know perfectly well just how far they can go in risking defiance of the dominance hierarchy, showing this by mischievous adventures within their group, in which they will sometimes apparently pretend to defy a senior or superior member of that group, running away unashamedly at the last moment and thereby acknowledging that in fact the dominance hierarchy may not ultimately be defied, although they are flexible and complex enough to pretend to challenge it, or sometimes actually to challenge it.

Man, of course, is the most complicated animal of all. But he is no more free from an inherent dependence on a dominance hierarchy built into his nervous system than any other social animal. Where his freedom exists in greater degree than any other animals is in his capacity *to be aware* of his impulse to place himself at a certain point in an order of status, a hierarchy of dominance, and to know or discover the rules, in whatever community he finds himself, for improving that status at the cost of whatever exertions may be necessary. Unfortunately it remains true that human society is by no means sufficiently flexible to allow as much mobility to its members as we would like to pretend.

When we are new-born, we have to learn our identity, and later our status: but if we believe that, at least in principle, all men are equal, reality soon teaches us, as George Orwell put it, that some men 'are more equal than others'. One more example of the inherent injustice of the human predicament though this may be, we challenge it at our peril, and in challenging it we meet the whole weight of the psychology of prejudice and persecution from our fellow men.

The first intimation of this may simply be relatively gentle social pressure; but if we resist that social pressure, we shall come up against hostilities, tensions, and frustrations, which, perhaps, had we not risked encountering them, we might never have dreamed existed. No man is born free of the capacity for prejudice. Aggressive self-assertiveness is present from birth onwards. It is fundamental, we cannot escape it, it is part of us just as the inherent built-in patterns of the nervous system are part of the complexless behaviour of domestic fowls or ants. Racial prejudice and religious bigotry are just two special examples of the way that we learn to rationalize our inherent dependence on dominance hierarchy, and the built-in prejudice in favour of our own comfort and self-esteem with which we are born. True, race prejudice has to be learned; religious bigotry has to be learned; but they can be learned only because they have an apt and inherent pupil in the prideful and instinctively self-willed aggressive aspect of each one of us.

Psychologically and sociologically, we can say that perhaps the soundest and most generally applicable theory to explain tension and hostility between different groups of human beings is what is called the frustration–aggression theory. When we cannot achieve what we want, when we are disappointed, when our hopes outrun our attainments, when somebody else gets the job, or the girl, or the money, we would like to be able to tell ourselves that it wasn't our fault; that they had an unfair advantage; that if we had started with whatever particular gifts or luck they had, or if they hadn't been around, we would have done better.

And, indeed, psychologically one and the same kind of mood and the same kind of frustration makes the thwarted child stamp the floor, the sacked workman kick his dog, the discouraged salesman blame his wife, the Gentile defame the Jew, the Jew despise the Gentile, the white man deride the Negro, and the Negro finally retaliate by proclaiming the need for Black Power or joining the Panthers.

Cruelty and bestiality in the way human beings treat one another are not always confined to those who have the upper hand, for we are all in this together; and we are all to blame. For the Christian, there is the echo of an old lesson here; for he is bound to recognize that man is of infinite value, but that in his human condition he is not, and never will be, perfect; that he comes into the world ready to be hateful and aggressive as well as to be loving and appreciative and kind. Little children are, indeed, born free from racial prejudice, but not from aggression.

But why should we be capable of such blindness, such smugness, and worst of all such unacknowledged hatred, when for so much of the time we truly believe that all we want to do is to live in peace and justice with our fellow men? I think one of the reasons is that we cannot bear to admit that others, different from ourselves as we see them to be, are as good as we are. We set too high a value on ourselves, too low a value on human beings as a whole: and this is the universal problem. Study the psychological development of the infant. The most important, the most fundamental need that the infant has after being born is to be able to differentiate himself from the rest of the world: between that aspect of his experience which is constantly part of him and, while ever-changing, goes with him wherever he goes, and that part which he comes to recognize as ineffably separate and distinct from him. His most fundamental lesson is in fact to recognize his own separateness, his identity, which he will later learn to call 'me': my body, my feelings, my thoughts, as something distinct from the whole of the rest of the world; which, infinitely varied, wonderful, packed with no matter what challenge, delights, or possibilities, is not 'me'.

This 'me/not me' differentiation is made instinctively, inevitably, and indeed of necessity, and where it isn't made, it may well be that normal development is impossible.

Writing more extensively about this in an earlier book,* I suggested that,

> ... consciousness defined as the total of subjective awareness at any instant in time, can for practical purposes be assumed to begin at birth. The infant's first response to this beginning takes a form which will always later be associated with overwhelming emotion, usually of a disagreeable kind; in fact he cries.
>
> What is happening at this instant, is that the baby's consciousness, which we can define as his subjective awareness of external reality, is being flooded with signals or sense impressions through every receptor channel between the periphery of his body and his cerebral cortex. ...
>
> It is the progressive integration and assimilation of such incoming stimuli, their correlation with each other, and the acquisition of patterns of experience made up of groups or sets of such stimuli having a constant relationship to each other, that forms the whole basis of learning, and of the development of the mental life of the individual. ...
>
> In effect, what the baby is doing is making a picture of the world and his place in it, out of this continual bombardment of sensory experience to which he is subjected during his waking hours; and

---

* David Stafford-Clark, *Psychiatry for Students*, Allen & Unwin, London, 1964.

> out of the constant and progressive sorting and assimilation of this experience, he becomes able within a matter of weeks or months to make some vitally important discoveries about himself and the world about him. . . .
>
> Probably his first recognition is that there is a part of life and experience which is permanently with him, and which later still he comes to recognize is actually part of him; and another part, constantly fluctuating and changing, which is in some way beyond and outside him. The distinction which the child may be imagined to be making at this stage, is between what is 'me' and what is 'not me'. . . .

Until we know that we exist in our own right we can't make our way in the world at all. Yet the mystics have always said, and the Eastern philosophers are always saying, that this really is the fundamental, the basic error of us all: that in truth man is one with the Universe, and that until he recognizes and achieves that sense of oneness and wholeness and reabsorption, he is never fully aware of what he is or what life is.

So we are kept stumbling along an expedient but ultimately tragic path: and part of our original sin is our original error, which yet paradoxically seems an absolute, inescapable necessity of our original existence.

Do you remember Housman's poem:

> Stars, I have seen them fall,
>   But when they drop and die
> No star is lost at all
>   From all the star-sown sky.
> The toil of all that be
>   Helps not the primal fault;
> It rains into the sea,
>   And still the sea is salt.

The primal fault: our loneliness, our individual uncertainty, our need for love and our proclivity for hatred; with this we come into the world and with this we are ready and raw material for suspicion, fear, hatred, prejudice, and all uncharitableness. Racial differences, real but biologically by no means dangerous differences, provide yet one more occasion for stubborn stumbling, for pride, for suffering, and inflicting pain. For every time we yield to prejudice, every time we insist upon our supreme distinction from other men, then whether or not we know or acknowledge it, our guilty hand is reaching for a stone. Can it be that although, in the Bible, God reminded us that he made us all from one mould, he has perhaps left it to us to discover just how difficult it is to live up to this as to so many other truths.

So we are once again back staring dumbly, and now perhaps almost incredulously, at our Bible. Significantly, it is open at the book of Ecclesiastes, Chapter 3, Verse 11. You will remember the ending of that verse: '. . . also he has put eternity into man's mind, yet so that he cannot find out what God has done from the beginning to the end'.

The next four verses are curiously, one might almost say ominously, authoritative, particularly in the context where they occur.

> I know that there is nothing better for them than to be happy and enjoy themselves as long as they live; also that it is God's gift to man that every one should eat and drink and take pleasure in all his toil. I know that whatever God does endures for ever; nothing can be added to it, nor anything taken from it; God has made it so, in order that men should fear before him. That which is, already has been; that which is to be, already has been; and God seeks what has been driven away. . . .

So, yet again, God is reserving the right to keep the final secret to himself. But we have to live it out, even, it would seem, to the end of time, without knowing why. If to ask why is a blasphemy, then it would be a paltry man who never blasphemed. But blasphemy by itself is an empty kind of defiance, and an even emptier act of love. What is demanded from us by God, says Jesus, is that we love him. The first commandment is quite explicit about this, and Jesus endorses it. The second is like unto it, and is 'thou shalt love thy neighbour as thyself'.

Is this then the message? That God needs our love but somehow cannot quite trust us with his confidence, although he trusted us with himself, or if you will, with his only begotten son, whom we fairly promptly killed? Can it really be that the only answer to this inherent cruelty – to this inescapable dominance hierarchy which is with us as surely as it was with the men of the Old Testament and of the New – the only answer to prejudice, is in an open unprejudiced love in the heart of each one of us; a love which must be openly acknowledged and fearlessly followed through?

It may seem strange that after all our examinations, after the sum total of our relentless inquisition, we should come back to the simple truth that only within the heart of each one of us lies the final solution at the human level. Somehow, we have to learn to love others as ourselves: unless we can do this, we not only doom others but are doomed ourselves. But if we can do this, there is no problem of racial or any other kind of prejudice which need overwhelm our judgement.

If we can only renounce our innate determination to regard ourselves as unique and of supreme importance, with everything else going to the wall, we can tackle this. But unless we are capable of this renunciation of self-centredness, then we cannot tackle it at all.

Love and humility are the only answer to this problem and they must be calmly and vigorously maintained in the face of prejudice, in the face of indignation; of segregation, of all arguments, all the answers about what is good and what is sound, and what is practical for society and so forth; because these answers and arguments are based ultimately on fear, hatred, insecurity, and the threat of being regarded as just like other people. Humility, then, and acceptance, are part of love; and love alone can pay the price for the abandonment of prejudice – and its natural outcome.*

The Jews must allow, not their customs to disappear, but their race to intermingle; so must the Gentiles; Negroes, Chinese, Arabs, Eskimoes, Caucasians must be free to marry and be given in marriage. The diversity of human races, which are simply a reflection of genetic flexibility and of cultural and geographical diversity, must not be segregated and kept apart but must be encouraged and enabled to unite. I believe this, and I put it forward as my personal answer, as a suggestion to meet, this enormous problem. And I end as I began: the roots of prejudice are not in the actual fact of difference, or in the supposed superiority or inferiority of one race to another; persecution arises not primarily out of bitter situations, not out of frictions of human proximity or distrust, which varies by distance, but simply out of the will of living man to think more highly of himself and less highly of others than he ought to think. The essential feature is the inescapable

* See Appendix Six, page 169.

self-centredness, separateness, and tragic personal pride of each individual one of us; whereby we do not love others as ourselves. If we can begin on that, we can begin at last to face, and then, perhaps, one day finally to solve, the problem.

As a statement of personal opinion and commitment to an attitude, that paragraph is unreserved and, I think, unexceptionable. As a contribution to knowledge, it may nevertheless be rejected by those who find this kind of knowledge unacceptable – for precisely the reason with which the paragraph deals. Ignorance can be deliberately preferred to knowledge where knowledge is uncomfortable. Invincible ignorance is not simply not knowing: it is not wanting to know.

To know in this context must imply to care. Knowing without caring is one of the most pernicious forms of self-deceit. But caring without knowing, or without facing the implications of knowledge, can be even worse. To attempt to grapple with *that* particular aspect of futile self-indulgence has been this book's particular task.

5

WHO'S TO DOOM

When the Judge Himself is Dragged to the Bar?

That question, you will remember, was in fact asked by a man who knew that he was doomed. And not only was he doomed, but the whole of his crew, who had signed on with him for something very different than the final disaster of the destruction of their ship by the terrible attack of the white whale, with whom Ahab had his final tryst. Ahab was doomed, his crew and his ship were all doomed; and only one man survives: the narrator of the story, who announces himself very briefly at the beginning with his opening words, 'Call me Ishmael.' Thereafter this narrator refers to himself only occasionally and indirectly, essentially as a witness of the fantastic and terrible story, which remarkably he unfolds. Only at the very end does he re-enter the action of the tale. But all are doomed save he, and he only is alive to tell the story.

In one sense, of course, he was doomed too, in that, like every other human being, by his birth he had entered into mortality. The doom of certain death lies upon each one of us that moment we are born, and by birth we enter into that. Although, as I have said, worship rather than reward is the theme of all the great religions of the world, the reward which most of them hold out is an escape from mortality; at the last, as Pizarro put it, the jailer will surely come and release us from the prison of time. But Pizarro's answer was definite, even while within his own heart he clung to the hope that the sun god would save his son King Atahuallpa, who reigned for him on earth just as he reigned as Eternal Father in Heaven. Pizarro did not confide even that flicker of hope, so soon to be extinguished by Atahuallpa's unquestionable extinction, like that of every other soldier whom Pizarro had ever seen die, at the end of Peter Shaffer's play, *The Royal Hunt of the Sun*. Dismissing immortality in his speech to the young Martin, Pizarro said, '. . . But, oh my boy, no one will come for all our crying. . . .'

Can it really be because we cling to the hope of immortality that we are moved to believe in the religion which promises it, and promises it explicitly and unequivocally, to those who do believe and whose lives are governed by that belief? Personally I doubt it. Indeed, I would like to think that human beings who hold and believe themselves to be truly Christian would try to live their lives after the example of him who they regard as their Saviour, even if they had no final hope of personal survival as the means of that salvation. If nothing awaited us beyond our death but an oblivion as complete, final, and infinite as that which, as far as we can tell, preceded our birth, surely that should make no difference to the way we act towards one another, to the values to which we subscribe, to the passion with which we try, as best we can, to seek what is right, and to stand up and be counted for it, during our mortal lifetime. If the pattern of our lives on this earth is finally governed simply by the hope of a joyful eternity, then it is both more fallible and more gullible than can be demanded, even if not always expected, from the best of what is in us.

Nevertheless, and in the teeth of all the evidence, hope certainly springs eternal within us. The resurgence of hope in fact has nothing to do with the evidence; everything to do with the need to be able to hope. Can we trust God's promises as they were given in the Old Testament? We have already seen that David learned in his lifetime that he could not. Can we believe that Jesus really knew what kind of a Father he had, and really understood the implications of that Father's incarnation in himself, as a God of Love? Leprosy, cruelty, and the trampling of the just by the unjust outlived Jesus, and they are far more evident in the world about us than was Jesus, even during his lifetime, outside the tiny circle of the globe in which he moved. A visitor from another planet would be more struck by the totality of the betrayal of the values and promises of the world's religions to their believers than by any evidence of their performance. But the most interesting thing is of course that we don't judge religions by their performance nearly as much as we continue to hope for their promises: even when perhaps the most inspiring hope is the hope, not for the rewards of eternal life, but for something far more tangible, far more real in their experience and beautiful in their imagination than any indefinite prolongation of personal existence could hope to be.

We are coming towards the end of this shared exploration. Before we part we need perhaps to examine for a little while the problems of time and eternity, honestly and objectively, as we have already attempted some examination of the problems of life's inherent injustice in the preceding four chapters. As I have said, the problem of time has interested me increasingly as a doctor and an observer as well as an admirer of the scientific method, particularly the integrity of scientific techniques in attempting to discover truth.* The scientist is perhaps at his most dependable when he is dealing pragmatically and empirically with observed facts as he sees them. The highest peaks of his attainment may still result from leaps of inductive imagination, rather than from pure deduction in the elaboration of scientific hypotheses.†

But just as the theologian must live within the rules he has constructed, and may even find his own faith circumscribed by them (as, for example, the devout Roman Catholic who says that we are bound to believe in hell because it is part of the fundamental appreciation of the Church's dogma, yet adds out of his humanity, and perhaps with a slightly sheepish smile, that although we are bound to believe in hell we are not bound to believe that our Lord has ever actually sent, or ever intends to send, anybody to be imprisoned in it for ever), so scientists too are sometimes imprisoned by the way they feel they must deal with the facts which they observe. The fact of time is one of these imprisoning limitations.

I shall not recapitulate my attempts made elsewhere to deal with this from a purely scientific standpoint: but it will certainly bear re-examination here from the standpoint of logic, and by way of illuminating the limitations of faith and imagination which the scientist imposes upon himself through some of his assumptions – not all of them

---

* See Appendix Five, page 165.
† Peter Medawar, *Induction and Intuition in Scientific Thought*, Methuen, London, 1969.

even fully acknowledged unless you press him hard on the subject – about the nature of time.

As Freud pointed out, there are two ways in which we can approach the nature of consciousness. First, we can study the apparatus through which consciousness is mediated: the entire nervous system and the signalling system which it serves, including its receptors from outside as well as from within the body and their activity in creating the actual images and sensations which make up our consciousness, together with our ability to recall them, which we term our memory, and our inability to escape entirely the influences of those which we no longer recall, but which have in the past affected us, which Freud called our unconscious mind.

Alternatively, said Freud, we can study the raw material of consciousness itself, as it is presented to us in our lives, and from its direct experience by other people, in what they tell us. In this sense, subjective consciousness, although the most important aspect of human existence at least at a material level, remains permanently and inevitably an isolated experience for each one of us. We may sympathize and give absolute credit to another's pain, but the only pain we can ever actually feel is our own. Pain is none the less real because of that. So it is, in a different sense, with time.*

We are all aware subjectively of the passage of time, and we can even begin to deduce at least some of the many rhythmic and repetitive activities of the nervous system and all the other biological clocks in the body which must be presumed to give us this sense of time. But it remains inescapably true that the only way we have of measuring

* See Appendix Five, page 165.

time, apart from our subjective sense of it, is by one form or another of the measurement of space. Whether this is space in the most obvious sense, like the movements of the hands over a clock face or the running of a tape or a film timed to last for a certain duration if run at a given speed, all time measurements outside our subjective sense seem ultimately reducible to space measurements. And this applies as equally to time as measured by radioactive decay or the vibration of caesium or quartz atoms as to the movements of the planets, or to the workings of the more obvious and conventional instruments which we employ as chronometers; to relate our own experience to those planetary movements which in turn divide our life into nights and days. What all these forms of measurement of time have in common, in addition to the fact that, apart from our subjective experience, they are indeed measurements of space, is that they are a series of logical sequences which can be repeated at will.

Now a series of logical sequences occur frequently in mathematics, and are readily recognizable as such and totally describable within the frame of reference of mathematical terms. Logical sequences which are used as measurements of time, however, differ in the world which is real to us from any other kind of logical sequence known to mathematics in that they are essentially one-way. They cannot be run backwards: in our experience they are ultimately irreversible.

> The moving finger writes; and, having writ,
> Moves on: nor all thy piety nor wit
>   Shall lure it back to cancel half a line,
> Nor all thy tears wash out a word of it.*

* *The Rubáiyát of Omar Khayyám*, translated by Edward Fitzgerald, LI.

Omar Khayyám was probably thinking more along theological and epistemological lines than making an observation about time itself. But it serves as well for the latter purpose as the former.

Any scientist worthy of the name must at some time or other ask himself why should this be so; and what would happen if it were not? He would then be led to attempting to postulate some sort of experiment, at least as a hypothesis, whereby an attempt was made to read the logical sequence of events in time backwards: not simply to predict the future, but, as it were, to predict the past, which could then be correlated with the past as actually recorded. Many scientists, confronted with this challenge, are as disturbed as theologians confronted by heresy. They have no right to be.

An intelligent medical student once answered a question I had put on these lines by saying that it was ultimately impossible to imagine us living our lives backwards so that we grew younger and younger and were eventually swallowed back into our mother's womb. But he made his point more by the ingenuity and imaginativeness with which he conceived of this possibility, only to reject it, than he did by offering any proof that in fact it was impossible. It is of course not impossible to construct a perfect visual record of exactly this event or series of events. All one would have to do would be to train a recording instrument, such as a film or television camera, on to the parents of the child as yet not even conceived, and, in the interests of scientific rigorousness, to keep it trained on them, like one of the longer and more relentless underground movies, throughout their copulation, the conception of the child, the mother's nine-month pregnancy, the birth of the baby, and the whole of that baby's life and growth into an adult up to the time of his or her death. Given such a complete motion picture record, it would then be perfectly possible to run the whole thing backwards, and to see him living his life in reverse, finishing up by returning to his mother's womb and ceasing to exist even there.

To conceive of this as a pictorial possibility is of course in no sense to prove that it could be done with time as we know it. Time as we know it can be, and indeed has to be, treated as though it were one more dimension of space in those mathematical relationships which enable us to understand the ultimate nature of the physical world. The space–time continuum is a mathematical necessity for the hypothesis of relativity; and probably, as far as our brains and minds are concerned, an ultimate absolute reality. But as our brains create or interpret it, and our minds conceive it, time is the one dimension in which travel can only ever be one way.

We can travel in either direction along any other dimension, but only from past into future along the time dimension. One might think that this staggering and unique property would excite more scientific curiosity than in fact it has. It seems rather to have been treated as a dogmatic axiom by scientists and mathematicians who would find it difficult to keep any kind of open mind about it. The whole concept of the storage and release of energy in the universe, the concept of entropy and the second law of thermodynamics, all of which are fundamental to the understanding which modern physics has reached of the nature of the universe, rest upon unquestioned acceptance of this one-way and one-way-only passage in time. Yet, seen in this way, Pizarro is right: time *is* a prison; and the concept of eternal life nothing more than a beautiful and ultimately inconceivable myth.

I began this book with a fragment of autobiography. Two more fragments press for inclusion as we approach its end. I shall relate them not in the temporal sequence in which they occurred, but will reverse it; not simply out of perversity in the light of the observations I have just made about time, but because the later of the two episodes, which I shall relate first, shows something of the mystery of human love in action, while the former, which will follow it, contains perhaps my only direct experience of a revelation of what divine love could mean.

The first incident occurred in the course of 1943, when I was the senior medical officer on a big British bomber base and had recently returned from a period of service on loan as a flying doctor with the United States Eighth Air Force in the United Kingdom. Several of my fellow officers who were pilots had also been involved in this rather agreeable period of Anglo-American fraternization, and one of them was a boy about the age of my brother; that is to say, about four years younger than myself. I was at that time twenty-six, so he would have been about twenty-two. My brother had in fact been killed two years previously.

Soon after I had returned from the American base to our own, my friend was detailed to take an aircraft on test with full bomb-load; and, as sometimes happened, one of the four engines of his aircraft failed at the moment of take-off, so that the aircraft slewed round, plunged back on to the ground and almost immediately caught fire. We were able to get to the wreckage very quickly to drag out those of the crew who were still alive, including the pilot, whose name I will call Graham. I had always had a particularly soft spot for Graham, because he reminded me so much of my brother who had been killed flying in the Fleet Air Arm barely two years before, a few weeks short of his own twenty-first birthday.

Graham was badly injured and terribly badly burned. One of his legs was charred right down to the bone of the femur, and the other was baked so that what remained of the flesh had split open; the whole lower half of his body had the terrible sickening smell of burned flesh. As he lay on the grass at the side of the runway I gave him the contents of three tubunic ampoules of morphia, which was all I had immediately available. I put each one of them straight into one of the veins of his arm, fairly confident that this would produce a sleep from which he would not awaken. It was quite obvious that he could not possibly survive the severity of these appalling injuries. But whereas I was right in the judgement, I was wrong about the immediate effects of this very large quantity of morphia given intravenously to a man in such terrible shock and pain. Its immediate effect was to kill the pain virtually instantly and to leave him clear-headed and, apart from his awareness that his burns must be very severe and his injuries possibly fatal, feeling no longer shocked or shattered. We lifted him on to a stretcher and took him gently back in the ambulance to sick-quarters, where we put him on to a bed in the emergency theatre while I prepared to set up a saline drip. He followed these preparations with interest, although I think we both knew that they were essentially a formality.

'What are you going to do now, Doc?' he said.

'Well,' I said, 'we've got you over the worst of your shock, now I'm going to put some fluid into you. We've telephoned the burns unit and when you are well enough to be moved we'll send you there in an ambulance and they'll take over.'

He looked at me steadily for a moment, and then he said: 'Come and stand beside me, Doc.'

I did so.

'Tell me the truth,' he said. 'I know what you've said is the right thing to say to somebody who is in my sort of shape but the truth is, I'm never going to leave this room alive, am I?'

I looked back at him. I think there were tears in my eyes, but if there were neither of us cared about that.

'No, Graham,' I said. 'I don't think you will leave this room alive.'

'Well then tell me, Doc, how long do you think it's going to take me to die, and is it going to hurt?'

'I'll see it doesn't hurt, Graham,' I said. 'We've finished with pain as far as you're concerned: and as far as time goes, I should say it will take about half an hour to an hour. You see, your vitality's pretty low, and although we can kill the pain with morphia, there's so much damaged tissue fluid in your circulation that it will kill you quite painlessly, without your knowing much about it. If there was anything else I could do, I would do it. You know that.'

'Yes,' he said, 'I know that. Everything seems very clear at the moment. I think there's just one thing I want to ask you.'

'Yes, Graham, what is it?'

'Doc, I want you to stand beside me and talk to me

about everything that we think to talk to each other about. The things I'd like to talk about my life, about the future that I won't have, and maybe there are some things you might want to say to me. And of course there are things I want you to tell my parents about me, after I am dead. But let's just talk together like two friends, and I want you to do something else for me.'

He bit his lip for a moment: the well-established British reserve was making its last appearance.

'I'll do anything you ask, Graham,' I said.

'Well I just want you to hold my hand, David,' he said (using my Christian name for the first time), 'and don't let go of my hand until I let go of yours.'

'All right,' I said, 'I'll do that and I won't let go until you do.'

About twenty minutes later, earlier perhaps than either of us had expected, he became finally unconscious, and a little while after that he was dead.

The point of this story is not that there is anything essentially unique either about the circumstances or the people. It is simply that, given this particular situation, this young human being was able to die with dignity, acknowledging and expressing his need to have a friend remain with him and yet going, as every man and woman must finally, to his death, alone. The act of dying is itself inescapably a lonely one, at least as far as we human beings can tell. But whatever dignity, peace, or comfort may be possible should be offered by whatever human love is available; and should not, incidentally, be compromised by too much peripheral and purely technical activity. There are many things that people sometimes feel they can or should do for a dying man. But unless these things add to the dying person's comfort, or at least do not detract from his peace and dignity and his capacity to communicate whatever he wants to say while he still has breath left to say it, they are not important. Drips, catheters, changing one tube for another, all these things must take second place to treating the human being as somebody who is about to take the last and most significant journey of all; and who can pause only long enough to say farewell to those he leaves behind and to hear them say a farewell to him.

As it happened, this man died in the sick-quarters on an R.A.F. bomber station, at the age of twenty-two, from some of the most terrible mutilating injuries and burns that I have ever seen. But even so, he died without pain and he died prepared as much as he could be for what death meant. He gave up the whole of the unlived part of his life without fear and, at the last, apparently without remorse, and he did this in the presence of a friend who loved and respected him, and through him so many others of his kind.

Which leads me to the second story. This concerns my brother's death, though I was not present when that happened. I learned of it through a telephone message, once again while I was on duty at the R.A.F. station where I was the doctor. My brother was four years younger than I was, his name was Jonathan, and we had always been closer to one another in companionship, affection, and understanding than either of us had been to anybody else, even our parents. David and Jonathan, and indeed those were our names. I think we lived up to those names in our own hearts. The war had been going about eighteen months and we were both in the services when he was killed. The training plane in which he was flying with another pilot pupil suffered sudden severe damage: one of its wings came off, almost certainly as a result of the impossibility of the Fleet Air Arm at that time maintaining totally adequate servicing of its training aircraft. Anyway, the immediate consequence was that the plane began to plunge vertically towards the ground. My brother was the senior pilot present and ordered the other man to bale out. He himself remained at the controls. By the time the other man was clear it was too late for him to save himself. He was killed instantly. I learned about this when my mother telephoned me at the airfield and told me. I knew what it meant to her and to my father; I was almost unable to bear to recognize what it meant to me.

But no matter how I felt, I had a very important job to do in the service for which I had volunteered; and now another responsibility to my parents, when I should see them. I had somehow to be able to help them to face and live through this loss, and yet I didn't feel I could do any of it. I was beaten. The person I loved most in all the world was dead; for me the world and life might just as well have ended too.

It happened that I had an hour to spare after learning of my brother's death, before I had to take part in a briefing for my aircrew.

I used up that hour by walking round the perimeter of the airfield by myself. I didn't know it then, but I was in one sense giving God his second chance with me. I put it in that arrogant way now, because it was how I felt at that time. I needed God's help and strength and support – but I couldn't forget my denials of him, nor could I understand what he could possibly do now. But I did open my heart to him. I prayed not for relief, but for endurance and strength to carry on with all the things I knew I had to do. I prayed not to seek death, but to be enabled to continue to live, if that should be my destiny. I stretched out my hand to God, hardly daring to ask or to believe, and during that hour, on that airfield, he showed me that he knew and cared.

I came back, not reconciled to my brother's death, not consoled; indeed, with much suffering, much agony still to endure, but with one thing certain – that God lived and cared, and once sought, could be found.

I suppose what finally determines whether or not someone is a Christian is what he believes; this must, in varying degrees, determine what he becomes. I claim nothing for what I have become; but from the time when, lost and unknowing, I asked God, whose very being I had denied, for help, and he gave it to me, I can never again doubt or falter in what I believe.

I wrote a short five-minute contribution to 'Lift Up Your Hearts' on BBC Radio in February 1957 about this. Reading it again now, I once again pause at the finality of that 'never again' in the last sentence. But in the sense of the basic feeling which prompted me to write this book and undertake the inaugural Nelson Lectures at Lancaster University, I must leave these words as they were written.

Looking back at my life in terms of my attitude to revealed religion I can see that, following the early encounters with the serpent, I eventually became an atheist shortly after my confirmation and for reasons directly connected with it. I hadn't completely understood that confirmation is the sacrament by which we confirm the promises to Christ made on our behalf by our god-parents.

I had expected it to be an occasion when God would bring home his presence to a willing believer. And so, having learned my catechism and done my part, when the actual moment came when the bishop laid his hands on me and I felt no fire from Heaven, no fluttering of the wings of the dove within my breast, I really began to doubt the whole thing. It seemed an anti-climax; and suggested to me that the whole thing was a polite fraud.

About the same time, I had begun to read Bernard Shaw, and his rationalist arguments against the existence of a personal God fitted in admirably with my mood of adolescent rebellion. And so I became not simply an atheist but a proselytizing atheist – ready to take up the cudgels of intellectual argument with any Christian prepared to discuss the subject with me.

I came back to belief in God because of my brother.

And there, plunging like the whale in my poem 'Pegasus', grappled to a wire, I suppose I have remained. Plunging and grappling with the contradictions of faith, hope, and charity, their promise, and so often it would seem a denial in reality. Faith, if it is there, cannot finally be denied, even though its expression may change and the outward forms of worship may cease totally as far as attendance at church or regular use or acceptance of the sacraments is concerned. Hope, likewise. Why else should I or any of my successors trouble, venture, or even dare to attempt the Nelson Lectures or books like this. We cannot live without some kind of hope, and since we do not choose to die without having ridden our mortal ticket to the end of the line, then we are bound to acknowledge the hope which somehow lives in us.

And the greatest of these three is charity. That was how

WHEN THE JUDGE HIMSELF IS DRAGGED TO THE BAR?

Jesus put it, the only Son of a loving Father who demanded of him and by him an atonement for all of us. How much irony, how much desperation there is in that simple statement. And although so little has survived for us to know of what Jesus said and did, we see him as a man transcending the limitations of mankind; in his extraordinary wisdom and love in the Sermon on the Mount, in his extraordinary love, courage, and ability to reach the hearts of even the most stiff-necked, obdurate and sadistic of his hearers when he delivered from their eager destructiveness the tired, dishevelled woman taken in adultery.* They were longing for a chance not simply to break up his meeting in the synagogue and enjoy the dreadful delights of a lynching, the public stoning of a helpless human being trapped in the judicial evil of the Mosaic law: they were exultant above all because at last they had caught this man, who called himself the Son of God, in a position in which he had either to deny the greatest prophet and law-giver of the Jewish people; or alternatively to stand by and watch one of the most hideous enactments of the cruelty of that law. And we can imagine Jesus thinking what to do, desperately and intensely, for a short while while he traced patterns in the dust with his finger: and then he turned to them and said, 'Let him that is without guilt among you cast the first stone.' And faced by that, not one of them could do it; and then he turned to her and said, 'Daughter does any man here condemn you?' and she replied, 'No Lord, no one.' And he said, 'Neither do I condemn you, go and sin no more.'

No suggestion that she hadn't sinned in the first place, no suggestion that it didn't matter: simply the certainty

* See Appendix Three, page 155.

that what mattered more was that he and his Father loved her, had forgiven her, and had shown it in an unanswerably perfect way.

Yet that same Jesus predicted no peace for the future. 'I come not to bring peace, but a sword' – and he was aware also of the implications even of that statement: 'They that live by the sword shall perish by the sword.' But could he ever have believed that his Father, the Lord and loving Father of mankind, created the world simply that it should perish, created mankind to love him and yet to lose the whole idea of love for ever; that is a proposition that I for one can never believe.

In September 1938, in one of the earliest poems I wrote, I attempted at the age of twenty-two to review the world as I saw it then, and as it seemed to me then to be headed.

PSALM FOR SEPTEMBER 1938

They have taken the scythe from the reaper's hands:
They have mounted him in a swift chariot:
No longer may he wander through the fields to harvest,
Now he must drive headlong.
Now he must plunge through the living host
With venomed swords bound to his chariot's wheels.
Now the smallest measure of his progress
Must be glutted with destruction.

See the cruel path that he has carved
Through all the warmth of life,
The golden haze of hope,
The cool shade of understanding,
The rich promise of peace.

See where the chariot's passing has laid waste
Past, present, future: crushed the heart of love,
Mangled the fruits of reason and endeavour:

WHEN THE JUDGE HIMSELF IS DRAGGED TO THE BAR?

Cast honour like carrion to the vultures.
And in the ruts made by the clumsy wheels,
Beauty lies dead: while misery, like mud,
Stifles the land. Rooted in hatred and deceit,
Despair, oppression, brutal injustice,
Are all that flourish now
In Spain, in China; and it may be here.

Whence then comes hope
For love, sincerity, and understanding?
From Christ, the Son of Man?
Where then is He?

When He was here we nailed Him to a cross:
Now He is gone, we crucify ourselves.
But if He lived, He would not scorn our cry.
Where is He now?

Even then, that was not just a rhetorical question. But in the days before our modern theologians in all their wisdom and deeply sincere enlightenment had begun to talk about noöspheres, and to dispute the whole concept of God, Heaven, or Christ as having any kind of temporal or material location, my question remained an open one, and remains an open one still. I do not know the answer to it, and now I do not know that I would even seek to know the answer to it in any terms that I could understand. The poem I have just reproduced owed something to an earlier poem of A. E. Housman, published posthumously, that I had recently read. It was called 'Easter Hymn', and was one of the posthumous collection of A. E. Housman's poetry, *More Poems*, made with his permission by his brother and published with a short preface some ten years before mine was written. On the title-page, before the actual collection begins, there is a fragment which

Housman's brother clearly regarded as appropriate to all that was to follow:

> They say my verse is sad: no wonder;
>   Its narrow measure spans
> Tears of eternity, and sorrow,
>   Not mine, but man's
>
> This is for all ill-treated fellows
>   Unborn and unbegot,
> For them to read when they're in trouble
>   And I am not.

A. E. Housman had often affirmed a certainty that death, if nothing else, was the end of trouble. That perhaps was his hope. His 'Easter Hymn' is a challenge rather than an affirmation of hope.

> EASTER HYMN
>
> If in that Syrian garden, ages slain,
> You sleep, and know not you are dead in vain,
> Nor even in dreams behold how dark and bright
> Ascends in smoke and fire by day and night
> The hate you died to quench and could but fan,
> Sleep well and see no morning, son of man.
> But if, the grave rent and the stone rolled by,
> At the right hand of majesty on high
> You sit, and sitting so remember yet
> Your tears, your agony and bloody sweat,
> Your cross and passion and the life you gave,
> Bow hither out of heaven and see and save.

What do all these affirmations, challenges, and truly troubled inquiries add up to? They add up to a necessity to examine whether all this is for nothing. Is it for nothing that we were born, that we live and that we die? Is it for nothing that we love and that we suffer? Is it for nothing that we have legends and mysteries? Is it for nothing that we pray? Is it to no one?

For myself (and in the last analysis for whom else can I speak?) it is not for nothing. I cling to the hope of love, the hope for all the world. That was the hope of Jesus, that is the hope of all religion. Truly for me, and I believe for all men, the hope of love is the only hope; the only foundation for belief. For me the hope of love is better than the certainty of justice.

APPENDICES

Introduction:
A Word of Warning

While this book was still in the planning stage, the publishers, who were also the sponsors of the Nelson Lectures, not unreasonably requested a brief statement of the author's aims and intentions for their own information and possibly for advance publicity. I responded with an 800-word statement indicating a fundamental concern with the mysterious injustice of the human predicament – admittedly only one aspect of the larger mystery of life itself. I saw as part of man's reaction to it all,

> ... an assumption that life cannot ultimately be without meaning or purpose. The search for this purpose may well be the basis of all religion; yet its discovery may never be possible: can this perhaps explain the necessity of faith as a foundation of religious belief?
>
> This suggested the first of the five questions; as well as the form of the book as a kind of compassionate inquisition, never straying too far from the basic postulate: for the human predicament remains for us at least the finally most crucial and poignant one, if only because we see it so clearly and so well. It is the predicament alike of the individual and of society: to be capable of perceiving what is ideal, and yet achieving only what the limitations of instinct, opportunity, and human vulnerability will permit; of conceiving what is good and yet achieving less and less of what is conducive to good. To aim high, to fall short, and to die without having reached one's goal, these are all aspects of our human state. And yet in our human state, they are perhaps all we can expect.

Yet, tragically and superbly defiant, we insist to the end upon expecting more. Whether our expectations include eternal life, or simply more satisfaction or relief in this one: whether we work, or pray, or look to sex, drugs, or violence for a release from despair, we are driven alike by some silent merciless necessity. This we must examine together in these lectures.

If it be true that the business of the scientist is to ask 'How?' and of the artist to ask 'Why?', then it will remain for us all to see what we can make of the answers. Our conclusion cannot finally exclude a belief in God, nor indeed need we exclude it: but neither need we rest content with the forms of belief as yet revealed to us. . . .

I intended the lectures to deal as well as I could with some of these expectations, contradictions, and escapes: I hope they did. But research and preparation for lectures inevitably involves more coverage of material than will ever finally get into them: and this is still true even of the background to a totally independent book, such as this. Appendices are one way of indicating the areas for further study or inquiry, if this has been stimulated, without impeding the even flow of the book as a whole.

The titles of these appendices are, in the main, self-explanatory: their content, while far from exhaustive, is sufficiently informative in places to have been suspected of being sensational. So read them only as and if you wish. Like the Bibliography, they are supplemental to the book.

APPENDIX I

Violence

Whatever else is obscure about Humpty Dumpty, it seems fairly certain that he was an egg. A real egg, too, the kind you buy from the dairy or the farm. This is why, after his tragic and violent experience of falling off the wall, he was irretrievably smashed. All the king's horses and all the king's men couldn't put Humpty Dumpty together again. And whatever the historical origin (round about the beginning of the nineteenth century), or the political allegory which this nursery rhyme may be believed to have contained, Humpty Dumpty's essential eggness is generally accepted as beyond question.

What makes this highly relevant to any one of us, men, women, and children alike, is that in one crucial sense we are all exactly like Humpty Dumpty; all eggs. The most essential and delicate structure of our bodies is compounded of a variety of fluid substances held together by membranes and supported by rigid or semi-rigid structures. Our skeleton is to the rest of us what the shell is to an egg. When we come to think of our brains, the means whereby we both experience and communicate the whole of our conscious lives, the analogy becomes even more painfully obvious.

For our skulls are indeed shells, enclosing the delicate fluid substance of our brains. Crack them hard enough, and our brains are damaged or even destroyed.

APPENDIX I

Though it is a fact much played down in fiction, drama, cinema, and television, a coshing, that is a blow on the head producing temporary unconsciousness but little else, *always and inevitably involves risk* of skull fracture or permanent brain damage. Blows on the head are never a joke: whether delivered by a truncheon, kitchen chair, bottle, loaded sock, or any other kind of cosh or blunt instrument.

A single knock out can tear brain membranes or destroy for ever tens of thousands of brain cells. Violence to the head remains an uncalculated, often unacknowledged, *but always potentially fatal*, assault.

When the outcome is intended to be lethal, the head remains the most obvious target. One particularly horrifying sequence in the amateur motion picture record of the assassination of President Kennedy (an 8-mm. film taken by a man called Abraham Zapruder, who simply happened to be training his camera on the presidential car from a favourable vantage point as it passed by, but who kept it focussed throughout the whole terrible event, until the car accelerated and sped towards the nearest hospital, with the president already fatally wounded, if not actually dead) shows the impact of the second bullet which struck the president's head. Whoever fired it, from whatever direction it came, it shattered the president's skull exactly like an egg-shell, and fragments went flying into the air.

That is the reality of violence, at once its greatest condemnation and a devastatingly indisputable vindication of its capacity to silence opposition. Of course, violence never proved anyone right or anyone wrong. We know that it never won an argument, but we know too that, made as we are, our flesh and blood and bones and nerves are sufficiently vulnerable to it for it to end an argument, and end it conclusively – simply by silencing the capacity of the victim to utter another human word, or think another human thought.

In one sense, therefore, it is the final brutal injustice of violence which makes it both so disgusting, and yet so implacable, when we seek to oppose it. Before attempting, however briefly, to see how it can be opposed, we must first steel ourselves to examine it a little further.

What are its personal origins? What are its aims? and what may be its achievements, no matter how deplorable their basis? Its most common origin is frustration. When all other natural outlets for the expression of feeling, of the assertion or even the awareness of our own identity and significance are suppressed, then we feel driven beyond endurance, and it is then that we are most likely to become violent.

This is as true of individuals living in oppressively impoverished, deprived, and meaningless backwaters of urban societies, overcrowded, lacking either privacy or any chance of peace or quiet, as it is of young mothers, cooped up in single rooms with squalling children. Frustration leads people to hit out, and whether they hit out at things or at other living creatures, at those weaker or stronger than themselves, the explosion into violence as the culmination of total frustration may be momentarily quite uncontrollable. The battered babies, brought into hospital by parents who 'can't understand' or 'can't remember' exactly what happened, are pitiful and sickening evidence of both the senselessness and helplessness of this kind of violence.

Deliberate calculated violence had other and even baser origins. And at its least evil, it may still be indefensible, the quickest way to bring a situation to a crisis or a conclusion, possibly, but never the best way; indeed, the use of violence against other living creatures is always finally an admission that their own integrity is to be sacrificed for some kind of expedience. Bullying or sadism come into a special category of their own, and a particularly repulsive one; moreover, they lack the spontaneity of true violence, which always contains an element of the totally unpredictable and immeasurable as an essential part of it.

As Norman Mailer put it,

> If a bully is beating up a friend who is smaller than himself, and knows precisely the point at which he is going to quit, that is not really an act of violence. That is simply excretion. That is why we despise the bully. But when violence is larger than one's ability to dominate, it is existential; then one is living in an instantaneous world of revelations. The saint and the psychopath share the same kind of experience. It is just that the saint has the mysterious virtue of being able to transcend this experience, while the psychopath is broken or made murderous. . . .

Violence can be said to have aims only when it is not purely an explosive phenomenon; when indeed there is something deliberate and calculating about it. Then the aims may be varied, but they are always essentially selfish: to increase personal prestige, to get something you can't get in any other way, whether it be money, power, or sex.

In this respect women are less naturally equipped for the use of violence than men, because, on the whole, they tend to be less muscularly strong. But this does not mean at all that they are less potentially violent in their feelings, or indeed in the way in which they translate those feelings into action if they get a chance. The legendary capacity of the women of very primitive tribes to finish off those captives who have survived a battle in which their side have been vanquished, can make as gruesome and appalling an impact as any other factual account of the effects of violence, from the explosions of bombs to the horrors and degradations of concentration camps.

In far less abnormal circumstances, violence can be enjoyed for its own sake by most of us, because the aggressive assertion of our own impact and identity upon the rest of the world represents the other side of the coin of frustration; and if we cannot do this by creative or constructive means, we may seek to do it, or perhaps vicariously to watch it being done, for the natural thrill it gives us, however despicable. Because this is a universal phenomenon we can follow it through its various gradations, from the comparatively healthy violence of the football field, through the more dubious bonds uniting crowds watching all-in wrestling, to the entirely contemptible but nevertheless by no means uncommon combination of curiosity and sensationalism which leads people to search avidly for the details of violent crimes in newspaper reports, or to watch street fights or riots from a safe distance.

Violence in varying degrees also plays a natural part in sex.* The bullying or teasing that can form a part of normal love-play or sexual petting, and can lead on to the final explosive pleasure of orgasm and momentary self-annihilation in sexual intercourse, differ more in degree than in kind from the violence of bites or black eyes in sexual fights between men and women, culminating perhaps in rape on the one hand, or a savagely painful and humiliating blow at the man's testicles on the other.

* See Appendix Three, page 155.

APPENDIX I

So prone are we to think in stereotyped patterns, unless we deliberately open our eyes to the wider truths which these conceal, that men may often think of violence as 'tough' and therefore masculine, while they think of sensitivity and delicacy as feminine, and therefore inappropriate in men, even though desirable in a condescending sort of way in women.

A fragment of autobiography comes to my mind as I write this. I can remember as a young medical student honestly believing that the vigorous and violent exchanges – not without their compensatory skill and satisfaction – which we used to enjoy while playing rugby football, were somehow mysteriously our own special kind of world; something which our girl friends, if they could be persuaded to endure the cold and discomfort to come and watch us, could never really know at first hand, safely ensconced as they were, wrapped up in rugs or fur coats and warm gloves in the stands or on the touchline. But the blood, sweat, toil, and tears which we might wring from our own exertions on the rugby field, paled by comparison with what I saw those same young women enduring, as part of the natural processes of their own lives, when they were giving birth to their children and I was learning the arts and crafts of midwifery by attending upon those labours.

Certainly, stereotyped thinking, or the fear of the naked truth which is so often the reason for such thinking, can play no part in the successful control of violence. The stereotyped answer is, of course, simply to repeat the crime. 'Give them a taste of their own medicine . . .' is the time-honoured and futile formula. This was the justification for hanging, drawing, and quartering on the one hand, and for flogging and the birch on the other. And yet every objective investigation into the truth of these matters which has ever been undertaken has always and consistently shown that to treat violent crime by violent punishment is simply to perpetuate and to increase violence in society as a whole.

It is true that because violence is an integral part of our human and animal nature, we cannot wholly escape from it; either by denial or simple and brutal retaliation. What we can do is, first, to accept its reality, and then individually to attempt to prepare ourselves for the fact that this reality includes us. We too must face the truth without being blinded by fear if we are to seek solutions.

The branch of medicine in which I have worked for the last twenty years has traditionally been associated with violence.* Violence arising usually out of the total frustration of the patients, who became victims, and formerly of those who looked after them, who were both afraid of and imprisoned by their task. This has begun to change in our lifetime, and the manner of its change could be an example to point the way to an individual solution of the problem of excessive violence in every one of us. If we can bear to accept rather than to fear other people, to recognize that even to suffer violence, if necessary to the point of risking or enduring a violent death without automatically thinking in terms of greater violence to protect ourselves, then we can go unarmed and without violence to meet the worst enemy which is contained within violence itself. We then can even share, and thereby begin to comprehend, that awful sense of ultimate helplessness, and the frustration and error to which it can lead.

* Frank London, *City Psychiatrist*, Four Square Books, London, 1956.

APPENDIX I

Nowadays patients with mental illness may no longer be thought of as wild animals, dangerous in themselves and deserving neither of safety nor compassion. Because all of us are built like eggs, all of us can be cracked or smashed. Violence in the end may still have to be constrained by force, but that force should be the gentle and comprehending power of human hands laid upon other human limbs; to prevent, rather than to incite, damage. V. S. Naipaul has pointed out that the greatest danger of pretending to complete objectivity about life and violence in other people is to reach an assessment of men, women, and children as 'mere anonymous flesh – and what statement can be made of mere flesh save that it has appetites and can be damaged?'

To see the essential value of human beings in terms of love and identification with them, rather than as objects to be exploited or denied, is to bring oneself within range of understanding violence which is within every one of us, which can indeed destroy every one of us; but whose understanding, if we can bear to share it, can give us a solution in which love can triumph over fear. But if ours is a God-given world, redeemed by an immortal Saviour, why does violence start with so many advantages; such as obviously achieved results, instant visual appeal, and (vicariously, or if personally successful) such pleasurable excitements? Not only would the devil seem to have the best tunes, but the more swinging accoutrements of power.

The final problem remains one of nurture; unfortunately, in this instance, in seeming opposition to nature. The idea of creative fun, or endeavour, has to be learned; the idea of destruction being fun in itself is inherent and instinctual. Children can as readily *learn* one as the other: but a taste for destruction comes more easily and spontaneously.*

* Witness the powerful allegory of the contrived ants *versus* scorpions battle set up by the children in Sam Peckinpah's opening sequence for his epic of decadent Western violence, *The Wild Bunch* (Warner Brothers/Seven Arts Production, 1969).

APPENDIX 2

Torture

The basic descriptions which follow are necessary for the reader who wishes to understand something of the essential brutality inherent in the persecution of heretics or those believed to be possessed by, or in league with, devils; in the Christian Church, from the Middle Ages up to the latter part of the eighteenth century. Brief as it will be, the material of this appendix is also disgusting and sickening and could well be omitted by the squeamish without discredit.

The most horrible thing about the persecutions and tortures undertaken by the various forms of inquisition, with the ostensible object of rooting out demoniacal possession and witchcraft, were not finally the frightful and sadistic ingenuity of the methods of torture employed: these are in all conscience bad enough; but all over the world, throughout the recorded history of mankind, for one reason or another people have found reasons for torturing their fellow men in frightful ways. What made this particular period and technique of torture and inquisition so indefensible was the infamous hypocrisy upon which it was based, and with which it was ritually carried out. The whole apparatus of judicial sanction was enrolled in this procedure, so that periodically the civil as well as the ecclesiastical courts were required to give judgements and pronounce sentences.

A typical procedure would be that a man or a woman would be suspected and then finally accused by their neighbours (or, in the case of priests, monks, or nuns, by those among whom they had worked) of either having entered into some pact with the devil (at the end of which, after some twenty years, the devil was held to be able to claim them and all their victims totally and for ever), or with having become possessed; sometimes through the agency of human instruments of the devil, sometimes (even totally innocently) by demons.

The belief in witchcraft and demonology which underlay all this, demanded comparably ritualistic exorcism, traces of which are still to be found in Prayer Books today. But in the 300 to 400 years during which this practice flourished in Europe, the entire procedure went through a number of stages, each one of which was incompatible with the ideals of Christianity or the concept of a God of love. The basic rationalization was that, without such Draconian measures, souls would be finally lost to the Saviour (compare Cardinal Newman, page 92).

Following accusation, evidence would be gathered and, for a while, the suspect would be allowed an uneasy existence, with a threat hanging over him or her but no specific action taken. At the whim of the witchfinders or other official agents of the inquisition, the victim would next be seized and summarily commanded to confess, usually to a complicated rigmarole of incantations and black magic rites; for example, celebrating the black mass, eating the flesh of new-born freshly murdered babies, drinking the blood of other sacrificial human victims, or indeed any combination of activities which the perverted imaginations of the persecutors could conceive. Whatever happened after this, there was no way out for the victim.

If they confessed (which they rarely did at first, because they tended to retain some flickering hope of justice or mercy if they renounced this paraphernalia of nonsense), they thereafter, as self-confessed accomplices of the devil, or possessed victims, had to be purged, executed, and their bodies burned to save their immortal souls. The tortures were given in this instance after the sentence of death had been passed, and so there was no need to preserve any chance of survival in the bodies of the victims. During torture it was customary to demand the names of accomplices, since these were a standard expectation of the inquisitors and witchfinders, who thereby kept themselves in business. Denunciations by the victim under torture of other totally innocent people, simply to gain some temporary respite, were remorselessly followed up.

At intervals, the victims would also be invited to confess, with the crucifix held before them; but even if they did confess in even greater detail than before, the tortures were liable to be resumed on the pretext that it was the voices of the possessing devils and not the victims' own true soul which was making the confession. Eventually, when the victim was clearly dying, he or she might be dragged on a hurdle through the streets in a state of terminal surgical shock; to be finally burned to death to complete the sentence, release the soul, drive out the devils, and serve as an example to everyone else.

The procedure was varied when the victim began by denying the accusations, in which case the first round of torture was necessary to extract a confession in place of the denial; followed by the trial of the still more or less intact victim, often naked and shaved all over the body so that devils' marks, such as warts or additional nipples, could be shown, and no chance left for small and presumably material little demons to hide in pubic hair, after which sentence was pronounced, and once again major tortures for the exaction of further confessions and lists of accomplices were undertaken. The outcome was always the same: death by fire (though hanging was acceptable in England), occasionally with final strangulation just before the flames were lit as a concession to those whose confession had eventually been believed.

What were these tortures like? It will be sufficient to indicate only those which have already been mentioned in the text, while leaving the details of the rack, the thumbscrews, the iron maiden, and the destruction of the limbs by shattering the joints with sledge hammers and wedges to the reader's imagination.

Strappado was an instrument used during interrogation, particularly to obtain confessions of the names of accomplices. With arms tied behind his back, the prisoner was hoisted to the ceiling by means of a pulley and at the same time heavy weights were tied to his feet until his shoulders were dislocated. During this ordeal it was customary to apply other minor refinements such as the thumbscrews or tearing off the nails with pincers. This was regarded as a preparatory torture for the major torment that was to succeed it – squassation: an extreme form of strappado. The prisoner was hoisted to the ceiling as before, but this time huge weights were attached to his limbs until his hips and knees as well as his shoulders and probably his elbows were dislocated.

He was left hanging in this predicament for a time, and

then the rope was released, only to be arrested with a terrible jerk a few inches from the floor, the shock of which was calculated to dislocate every remaining joint in the body and fracture many of the bones. Four applications of squassation were regarded as the equivalent of the death sentence; although, whether the victim was still alive or dead, the public dragging through the streets on a hurdle and the final burning were rarely omitted.

Burning might take place over a pyre of logs (standard procedure), or occasionally over a slower fire made of brushwood, to prolong the torment. Strangulation for the lucky few whose confession had ultimately been accepted took place after the dragging through the streets and before committal to the flames.

It is necessary to remember that all this was done in the name of a loving God, and to save souls for a Christ who had already himself been tortured to death as man's redeemer.

APPENDIX 3

Sex

The literature on sex throughout the history of the world is vast, and by now virtually omnipresent. I do not intend to attempt to add to it here, but merely to draw from a few personal observations to make the point that its transcendence in the language of the religious mystics is apt to be no less banal than the ultimately humourless, ludicrous, and grotesque presentation of what is called hard pornography; which is really an attempt to supply the pleasures of sexuality by dwelling on its natural failures, alternatives, and perversions.*

Once more, nature is revealed as unbelievably wasteful and profligate. While endorsing George Santayana's observation about nature, and those strictures quoted from Sherrington in the main text (pages 10-11), we are again reminded that the natural answer to the failure of even the most delicate and wonderful process in the functioning of nature herself is simply to provide for such a vast expenditure of life and effort that somehow, somewhere, some of it is bound to come out right. That this condemns so much else to failure and degradation, seems, within nature, to be of no importance whatever. Here again the loving Father

---

* Cf. *The Language of the Mystics: The Practices of Flagellants*' (religious no less than sado-masochistic). *The Devotions and Diaries of St. Theresa of the Little Flower.*

of mankind and his sacrificed Son are mocked at least at the level of our human perception, by their own creation.

Readers wishing to pursue this aspect of the matter further in literature for which I personally have been responsible can turn to the Foreword of *The Undergrowth of Literature* (main text by Gillian Freeman), a book published by Nelson (London, 1967). Four other relevant essays constitute the author's literary contribution to this subject apart from essentially technical and professional work in text books and source books. They comprise two articles in *Nova* (1966), one in *Christian Action* (Autumn 1966), and one for the summer edition of *Twentieth Century Magazine* in 1965.

An admirably clear and relevant treatise for the intelligent layman which cannot be omitted is Anthony Storr's Pelican *Sexual Deviation*.* His comments on sadomasochism are apt and quotable:†

> ... Swinburne wrote a work entitled *Sadopaideia* which describes how an undergraduate was 'led through the pleasant paths of masochism to the supreme joys of sadism'; and his poem *Dolores* is an impassioned hymn to sado-masochism which contains some of his best-known lines.
>
>> Could you hurt me, sweet lips, though I hurt you?
>> Men touch them, and change in a trice
>> The lilies and languors of virtue
>> For the roses and raptures of vice;
>> Those lie where thy foot on the floor is,
>> These crown and caress thee and chain,
>> O splendid and sterile Dolores,
>> Our Lady of Pain.
>
> It is very characteristic of persons who are sado-masochistically

---

* Anthony Storr, *Sexual Deviation*, Penguin Books, Harmondsworth, 1964.
† See also Appendix One, page 141.

inclined both to attempt to justify their interest, or to imagine that it could find fulfilment in some more tolerant age than the present. De Sade, in his political writings, advocated a future régime in which every citizen should be free to practise any deviation to which he was inclined; while Swinburne turned to the past and imagines a pre-Christian era in which his own tastes were accepted.

> Thou wert fair in the fearless old fashion,
>   And thy limbs are as melodies yet,
> And move to the music of passion
>   With lithe and lascivious regret.
> What ailed us, O gods, to desert you
>   For creeds that refuse and restrain?
> Come down and redeem us from virtue,
>   Our Lady of Pain.

The influence of sado-masochism can be detected in the writings of many other authors who do not admit, or perhaps even recognize, their inclination. It is impossible, for example, to read the short stories of Conan Doyle, or the libretti of W. S. Gilbert, without becoming aware that pain held something of a fascination for them; and even the poet Tennyson admitted an interest in de Sade.

People who consult a psychiatrist on account of sado-masochistic impulses are, predictably, those who are ill-at-ease with these impulses. There are many, however, who do not try either to suppress their desires or to alter their direction; and those who cannot find a willing partner in spouse or lover buy what they want from prostitutes who keep a supply of whips, racks, manacles, and other devices to comply with their clients' requirements. It is rare to find either sadists or masochists who have inflicted or received serious physical injury, although extensive bruising occurs in a few instances, and the writer has seen one woman who was alarmed by the severity of the damage which she had herself invited from her lover. Proust's description of the chaining and flogging of M. de Charlus in a Parisian brothel does not exceed what may sometimes actually occur; but the majority of the sado-masochistically inclined, in acting upon their impulses, do not go beyond comparatively mild forms of beating. Phantasy, however, has no limits; and

APPENDIX 3

in de Sade it is possible, though rapidly tedious, to read of tortures and murders galore. De Sade spent much of his life in prison; but his physical confinement did not have the effect of restraining his imagination, and, in his phantasies, he makes no attempt to conform to the limitations of reality.

To the civilized eye, nothing appears more incongruous with love than the desire to hurt or be hurt; but, at a physiological level, all human passions are closely linked, and love and pain are less disparate than liberal humanists may like to think. The behaviour of people who are in the throes of sexual excitement is indistinguishable from that of people in severe pain. As Kinsey says: 'In the most extreme types of sexual reaction an individual who has experienced orgasm may double and throw his body into continuous and violent motion, arch his back, throw his hips, twist his head, thrust out his arms and legs, verbalize, moan, groan, or scream in much the same way as a person who is suffering the extremes of torture.'

Freud's discovery that a small child who witnessed sexual intercourse between adults was likely to interpret it as an attack by the man upon the woman is scarcely surprising. It is to be expected that an encounter so passionate would be associated with violence and hurt in the mind of a child whose experience of coming up against other bodies in a forceful way has hitherto been only painful. For sexual intercourse is the only habitual human activity in which two bodies can be forcefully engaged *without* causing pain to one another. We all interpret the unfamiliar in terms of the familiar; and some children who discover that beating or other sado-masochistic practices such as tying each other up are sexually exciting, are undoubtedly substituting an activity which is known and comprehensible to them for one which is still mysteriously remote from their actual experience.* Such interests persist in those who, because of sexual inferiority or guilt, have been unable to make a mature love-relationship; so that the sado-masochistic practice or phantasy carries the emotional charge which is felt by the normal person to belong to sexual intercourse.

---

* See Suzanne Lilar, *Aspects of Love in Western Society*, Thames & Hudson, London, 1965 (author's footnote).

Some of those for whom sado-masochistic practices have a peculiar fascination seem to be trying to reach an intensity of sexual experience of which they have an inner imaginative picture but which they cannot find in love-making unaccompanied by painful stimuli. In such people there is an internal embargo on the passionate aspect of love, so that love-making is too gentle and too tender to be wildly exciting. Paradoxically, the sado-masochistic person is often over-anxious not to hurt or to be hurt by his partner, and so may be less than normally forceful or yielding in the act of love. The sado-masochistic phantasies and actions which attract him are compensations for this lack of passion – ways in which he can reach the intensity of erotic experience which other, less inhibited men reach naturally during the sexual act.

It is only when sado-masochism is extreme or divorced from sexual intercourse that it can be counted a deviation. For countless couples engage in minor sado-masochistic rituals which serve the purpose of arousing them erotically, and are thus valuable introductory steps to the sexual act itself. Are there any two lovers who have not played some version of the age-old game in which one dominates and the other submits, or who have not teasingly tormented each other by pretending to kiss and then withdrawing? Such games may seem remote from the floggings of a de Sade or the humiliations of a Sacher-Masoch, but both spring from the same fundamental roots.

APPENDIX 4

Drugs

Go, go, go, said the bird: human kind
Cannot bear very much reality.
– T. S. ELIOT, 'Burnt Norton', *Four Quartets*

Why do ants alone have parasites whose intoxicating moistures they drink, and for whom they will even sacrifice their young? Because as they are the most highly socialized of insects, so their lives are the most intolerable. . . . How do savages all over the world, in every climate, discover in frozen tundras or remote jungles the one plant, often similar to countless others of the same species which could, only by a very elaborate process, give them fantasies, intoxication, freedom from care? . . .

Opium smokers in the East become surrounded by cats, dogs, birds, and even spiders, which are attracted to the smell. The craving for the drug proceeds from the brain cells which revolt and overrule the will. . . . Peyotl, one of the rarest and most obscure drugs, yet gave its name to the range of uninhabited mountains where it was found – CYRIL CONNOLLY ('PALINURUS'), *The Unquiet Grave*.

Like the literature of sex, the literature on drugs and intoxicants has also proliferated overwhelmingly in the last ten years. Once again setting aside technically professional communications, I might draw the reader's attention to three articles I wrote for *The Times* on the subject, on 17 February and 11 and 12 April 1967 respectively. They included the quotations which head this appendix. These, in turn, highlight one of the reasons why people take drugs; simply to make some of the anguish, which it has been our task to explore in our examination of the human predicament in this book, less intolerable.

The other reason may be derived from the name given by some devotees to some of the drugs concerned, namely 'psychedelic'. This name is derived directly from the synthesis of two Greek words, and means, in loose translation, mind-expanding or mind-releasing drugs. Doctors regard so-called psychedelic drugs as hallucinogens or psychoto-mimetic preparations; names used in turn by members of the medical profession to refer to the attribute possessed by such drugs to bring about changes in the biochemistry of the brain, and therefore in the environment of the mind. Such changes correspond more to the experience of severance from reality of the kind encountered in certain forms of mental illness than to any normal waking experience encountered in the day-to-day life of healthy human beings.

From this it will be clear that, to regard a drug as a hallucinogen, is to look at it from the standpoint of a doctor who may still use it in research or treatment: whereas to regard it as the bearer of a psychedelic experience is to belong to that section of opinion which considers such drugs a blessing to mankind comparable to the wine and opium of the ancient Greeks, the reconcilers to living and dying presented to man by Dionysus and Morpheus, capable of enriching life and enobling death by transcending the human limitations of existence.

No serious and responsible consideration of drug-taking, today or at any other time, can leave alcohol out of consideration. For alcohol is indisputably a serious and potentially damaging drug: it was once described by

Professor Aubrey Lewis as, '. . . so permissible and trusted a poison, so easy of access for those who wish to escape from their troubles, that it is resorted to in excess by maladjusted persons of every type. . . '.

It is also a traditional balm or anodyne, taken for precisely the same reasons that marijuana and barbiturates are taken by those who prefer them as a day-to-day indulgence. It is not only more dangerous than marijuana, but at least as liable to create dependence in many people as barbiturates, were the latter to be equally available as an alternative.

Much has been written and said about the effect of all these solvents of experience, whereby the inability or disinclination of human beings to bear very much reality can find a partial and always treacherous solution in an escape or distortion of reality by some form of chemical interference with the function of their nervous apparatus. This is the final common factor shared by all such drugs, including alcohol; even by tobacco, whose ultimate dangers are different but probably no less damaging.

They impart a spurious comfort, at the price of producing an insulation, at least temporarily, from some of the slings and arrows of outrageous fortune. If we accept as indisputably true that social abuse of heroin and cocaine is desperately dangerous, while that of *Cannabis indica* carries nothing like the same risks, where on the scale of social menace are amphetamines, LSD,* alcohol, and barbiturates? The only honest answer must be somewhere between these two extremes.

It remains an indisputable fact that whereas some intoxicants are an undiluted curse, none is an unmixed

* Lysergic acid diethylamide: a powerful hallucinogenic drug.

blessing. Human beings, as a whole, continue to seek them because they are solvents of the harsh impact of reality; rather than because they reveal a deeper truth. Nevertheless there have been distinguished proponents of the psychedelic theory, among whom was Aldous Huxley, whose book *The Doors of Perception* suggested that man's consciousness was normally blinkered like the eyes of a sensitive horse, to prevent distraction by the innumerable direct and indirect experiences of reality which might otherwise swamp man's willingness or capacity to concentrate on the simple task of living. To take a hallucinogen, said Huxley, is to remove the blinkers, open the doors of perception, and to gain the kind of insight which might only otherwise come as part of the revelation of a mystical experience; and then only to the chosen few who have forsaken all else to discover it.*

Since it is obviously very much easier to take a few drops of a colourless liquid or a small capsule than to undergo the self-discipline of the life of a mystic, with its emphasis upon seclusion, contemplation, and asceticism, it is clear that there is likely to be considerable popular appeal about the indiscriminate use of hallucinogens in general, and mescalin and LSD in particular. LSD is in fact comparatively easy to make, and until very recently was fairly freely available on prescription to any doctor who had use for it.

But despite its relatively enormous kick in terms of

* Huxley's introduction to mescalin occurred in California 'on a bright May morning in 1953', when he participated as 'a willing guinea pig' in an experimental observation of the effects upon him of 'four tenths of a gramme of mescalin dissolved in half a glass of water . . .'. The physician conducting the experiment was Dr Humphrey Osmond, a graduate of Guy's Hospital, currently working in Saskatchewan.

APPENDIX 4

sheer impact (a thirty millionth of an ounce can turn the senses inside out; sounds may be seen, colours heard; and experienced or adventurous users of the drug may increase this dosage five to ten times), LSD remains no miracle drug, nor has it yet been proved to produce more lastingly favourable results in medicine in general, or psychiatry in particular, than other drugs properly used in combination with other appropriate medical and nursing techniques. It certainly has a place in the broad spectrum of psychiatric research, both physiological and psychodynamic; but more than that no one can say.

What *can* be decisively said at this stage is that the revelations claimed by proponents of the psychedelic revolution have proved, on further scrutiny, to be neither revealing nor revolutionary. Their paintings have no special quality, their writings no special insight or illumination. In short, the place of LSD would seem to be indisputably in the hospital or the laboratory; not in the home or the beat club, nor even in the temples of the new philosophy which rests upon the psychedelic revolution in the United States.

APPENDIX 5

Time

Reprise.

> That prison the Priest calls Sin Original, I know as Time. And seen in time everything is trivial. Pain. Good. God is trivial in that seeing. Trapped in this cage we cry out 'There's a jailer; there must be. At the last, last, last of lasts he will let us out. He will! He will! . . .' But, oh my boy, no one will come for all our crying. . . .

No one is obliged to agree with Pizarro, although he speaks so eloquently through Peter Shaffer's words. I do not personally see the idea of God as trivial within the framework of the concept of time. But that concept has fascinated me for a long time, and I have both read and written about the subject. The Bibliography includes source books and references upon the subject of time.

For scientists and mathematicians, time has always provided a particularly fascinating challenge; its nature, the ways in which it resembles the concept of space and the ways in which it differs from it. But few scientists have found any particular difficulty in conceiving of time extending into infinity: the scientific equivalent of the concept of eternal life. Some have even believed in that concept, and specifically in the survival of the soul after death; although more as a personal and idiosyncratic conviction than as an outcome of their scientific observations and experience.

One fellow of the Royal Society, Sir Oliver Lodge, was a convinced spiritualist. Before his death, he promised to put into practice the simple scientific experimental verification of his hypothesis that we survive bodily death, and should be able to communicate with those interested to listen for our signals, after we have become immortal. Sir Oliver Lodge has been dead for thirty years, but no one has heard from him yet.

In the professional work of the mathematician and scientist, the concept of time as another and invisible dimension of space (often referred to as the spatialization of time) has proved of immense value in laying the essential foundations for the general theory of relativity. The full concept of the four-dimensional space–time continuum of Minkowski was introduced by him with the now-famous words: 'Henceforth space by itself, and time by itself, are doomed to fade away into mere shadows, and only a kind of union of the two will preserve an independent reality' (addressing the 18th assembly of German Natural Scientists and Physicians in Cologne, 21 September 1908).

In mathematical theory, such spatialized time, or indeed any measured period of time, can be expressed as a logical sequence. But logical sequences in mathematics are reversible: time, at least in human experience, is not. We know neither its direction nor its rate. We only know that, from the time we are born, it is carrying us remorselessly to the day when we will die. It is therefore not surprising that, at a human level, for many people the idea of an eternal life after death has seemed so important.

I want here only to ask the simple question of what kind of life this is supposed to be. It is most definitely a part of the Christian message, is believed to be what

Christ entered into after his crucifixion, and what awaits all of us, after our death, and presumably in some further modified form, after the day of judgement. But here the confusion between the traditional Judaic concepts of judgement and atonement and their Christian counterparts begin to seem confusing, at least to other than theologians. Sparing ourselves that confusion, we can still ask what kind of life is eternal life supposed to be.

We have been told that it is a disembodied life in the human sense, and specifically that there is no place in it either for marriage or giving in marriage. It becomes increasingly difficult to take seriously a concept of an eternal life which bears absolutely no resemblance to any kind of existing life that we have known. How old would we be in that life to come – the age we are when we die, the age we were when we were at our prime, younger, older, capable or incapable of learning or developing from the timeless existence in which we will live for ever?

If one tries, however briefly, to form a concept of this eternal life, in which everyone who ever lived continues to live indefinitely but in a totally inconceivable fashion, with neither age, sex, maturity, nor human limitations any longer operative, the whole concept becomes a recognizable impossibility – a nonsense, as the logical positivists would remorselessly affirm.

Pizarro knew of this difficulty: and once again his words express it perhaps as well as it can be expressed:

> Listen, listen. . . . Everything we feel is made of time. All the beauties of life are shaped by it. Imagine a fixed sunset: the last note of a song that hung an hour, or a kiss for half of it. Try and halt a moment in our lives and it becomes maggoty at once. Even that word 'moment' is wrong, since that would mean a speck of time,

something you could pick up on a rag and peer at . . . but that's the awful trap of life. You can't escape maggots unless you go with time, and if you go they wriggle in you anyway.

With humility, but after considerable thought and with profound personal conviction, I can only say that for me an existence in which time itself has ceased to exist is not only inconceivable, but would seem to be meaningless: as such I cannot hope for it, still less believe in it.

APPENDIX 6

'If I Were a Carpenter ...'

If I were a carpenter
And you were a lady,
Would you marry me anyway?
Would you have my baby?

These are the mysterious words of a slightly mysterious popular song which has hovered on the fringe of the charts for the past two or three years.* Its tune is certainly traditional; and the most recent words and version are probably its only contemporary aspect. I have found them interesting from the time when I first encountered them, because they serve so pointedly to illuminate the cross-tensions which can develop between love, status, and the ideals of justice.

The opening verse is quoted above: but there are a number of other verses in which the singer asks what his chances would have been if he were a tinker, a mill-wheel grinder, and a number of other occupations, all of them crafts tinged with a medieval flavour, and invested in this age with an implication of proud, defiant loneliness.

But the first verse will serve to put this entire communication in the context in which we can best examine it: disturbing, emotional, and yet insistent upon something

* 1970.

extremely human, and extremely fallible. It is indeed an extraordinary song, and its tune alone might have gained it considerable popularity if its words had not been just sufficiently uncomfortable to exclude it from the caprice of total popular acclaim.

'If I were a carpenter . . .' This suggests that, whatever he is, he isn't a carpenter. And it also suggests something else, that whatever he is, he imagines that what he is is better than a carpenter. A very human, very dangerous, very alarming, very characteristic assumption.

The second line: 'And you were a lady . . .' – same assumption: she can't be.

The third line: 'Would you marry me anyway?' – presumption being that she looks like marrying him the way things are, whatever that is.

The question is, would she still feel the same way about him if these other conditions of her being a lady and his being a carpenter prevailed? Final question: 'Would you have my baby?'

The nub of this interrogation is, does she really regard him as a human being, will she love him and commit herself to him whatever happens? But why the carpenter, to begin with? After all, the carpenter is a skilled tradesman, and a man would have to have a very self-conscious and disturbing sense of inferiority, or a very high degree of snobbishness (which often comes to the same thing), if he were to presume that, whatever he was, being a carpenter would be so inferior to it that a woman who loved him would spurn the carpenter where she would accept the man as he is at the time of this questioning.

In fact what he is is never revealed in the song at all. But the association to the idea of a carpenter begins inescapably to involve once again the carpenter of history, Jesus of Nazareth. If only the last three years of his life were spent in what has been called his ministry, culminating in his execution, then he must have spent some time first as an apprentice and then as a carpenter* before becoming what may well have seemed, at least at first, a dropout, a profitless vagrant. Historically, being a carpenter has in fact an almost impregnable respectability; and to choose it as an example of a demeaning occupation, which might lead a woman in love to change her mind about her lover, is obviously inept. So obviously as to suggest that it was deliberately ominous. For not only is the questioner clearly not a carpenter, but equally clearly he believes he would be less attractive a proposition if he were. So he is very unsure about his status, both in the eyes of the world, and in the eyes of the woman.

Could his question be, 'If I were like Jesus, as misunderstood and apparently misleading to so many people, would you still want to marry me and have my baby? If you were in a position to choose [which perhaps is what being a lady means in this context], or could discriminate against those not good or gentle enough for you, would I still be the one you'd want?' The ominous nature of the inquiry persists throughout the following verses, through which it becomes increasingly clear that the singer is implying that he is not really satisfied about the depth of love, or the extent of recognition of his humanity, that he is receiving. To prove her dedication to him, the wretched girl will have to follow him, walk behind him, put up with various other incidental indignities inseparable from their joint way of life; and described by him with a mixture of proud and

* cf. anecdote in Slaughterhouse 5 (op. cit.) pages 174-5.

APPENDIX 6

surly relish, and a resentful expectation of the world's contempt; all this against the insistently querulous background of his own doubts about her loyalty and constancy.

In fact, the questioner is half-humble, half-arrogant, seeking to become sure of himself and of the woman, basically unsure whether he can be. This is indeed the situation of a man whose humanity is in question, not necessarily for any reason which he can control; and the attitude which it evokes in him is characteristic of the attitude of human beings in that kind of predicament.

Certainly there is no justice in this: but then there is no guarantee of justice in life itself. Prejudice of any kind is an inherent denial of justice; and when prejudice is defended by such sickeningly familiar phrases as 'keep politics out of sport', what in fact is meant, whether or not it is acknowledged, is 'keep justice out of politics'. Racial prejudice is only one of many kinds of prejudice and snobbery which lead to indefensible cruelties and leave their victims not only often totally helpless, but bitter and hopeless, hopeless and recriminatory. Because finally it is their humanity which is being denied.

> If I was your neighbour man,
> And was black from a baby,
> Could you see me as human at all
> Or would you just say maybe?

And that perhaps is the worst of it: the 'maybe'. The continuing uncertainty, the fact that today your humanity may be acknowledged in one situation, while yet tomorrow it may be denied in another; and that if you protest, the attitude of most of the human beings in your immediate environment may well be neither one of sympathy, nor even of hostility, but simply of a kind of nerveless indifference; they would prefer not to know: they just don't want to.

But a man's humanity is not something that he can continually expose to have either accepted or spurned like a dubious cheque; it is something which, for him, must be recognized if life is to be bearable; and from where any individual stands, he cannot willingly risk, still less accept or concede, the right of anyone else to deny that humanity. But for their part, those who would deny it would prefer not to know that they are denying it; not to acknowledge that the problem exists. Even that determined ignorance, and its devastating consequences, can be detected in the pattern of the song.

EPILOGUE

by Professor Ninian Smart

The study of religion is being recognized as of increasing importance for the understanding of human culture, society and psychology. By 'the study of religion' I mean the attempt to describe, explain, and understand religious beliefs and behaviour – rather than that other (quite legitimate) activity going by the name, 'Christian theology', which is the scholarly attempt to systematize and articulate a particular religious viewpoint. The study of religion is bound to involve many disciplines – history, philology, sociology, philosophy, psychology, and so forth.

The present book, which formed the basis of the Nelson Lectures in the University of Lancaster, is by an eminent psychiatrist. This means that its principal concern is with the psychology of religion. It is especially valuable because of the need in this country, where the psychology of religion is underdeveloped in our universities, to approach religion from the direction of the insights of psychology – and of psychiatry in particular. Some important works in the psychology of religion are mainly descriptive – consider Evelyn Underhill's work on mystical experience or more recently Marghanita Laski's *Ecstasy*. Other works are more speculative and philosophical, such as William James's *The Varieties of Religious Experience*. Others again belong to social psychology: consider Michael Argyle's

Religious Behaviour. And we are all of us aware of the crucial psychoanalytic traditions – the works of Freud, Jung, Adler, Fromm, and others. Dr David Stafford-Clark's approach naturally belongs in this latter category: and the University of Lancaster was singularly fortunate that he should agree to open the series of Nelson Lectures. His noted contributions to the exegesis of Freud, his reputation as a psychiatrist and his well-known breadth of interest as writer and broadcaster are sufficient to guarantee him an attentive hearing.

I spoke above of the study of religion. In an important sense it must be scientific. But obviously the precise procedures of the natural sciences cannot be woodenly applied to the understanding of human behaviour, feelings, and institutions. It is, for example, necessary for the student of humanity to enter into the perspectives of those whom he studies – yet an electron or a gene has no perspective of this kind. Because of this fact, the study of religion needs to be imaginative, in the special sense that imagination is used to understand the consciousness and intentions of others. Not only the behaviour of men counts, but also their ideals and sentiments. We must look not only to the forms of practice, but also to the content of aspirations. It is not therefore surprising that Dr Stafford-Clark, in his explanation of the tension and contradiction in men's experience of the world and of what lies 'beyond' the world, should have adopted an imaginative, poetic approach to the subject dealt with in this book. This is one reason why the book is difficult to put down, for it moves forward from one image and argument to another.

At first sight this makes the theme of the lectures oblique. Yet the obliqueness has an important point. Just as the novelist may be saying something universal through the description of the particular, so the evocation of religious attitudes and sentiments and of their underlying psychological dramas cannot be done flatly, straightforwardly. One important thing which we must remember is that religions and ideologies are more than systems of metaphysics or analysis. They engage men in an existential world-view, and many of their tensions arise from the need to align values with realities and feelings with facts.

It is presumptuous of me to attempt to present Dr Stafford-Clark's main argument; and I only offer the following account of a main strand of his theme as a means of raising questions. If I distort his drift, the fault is entirely mine.

In this book Dr Stafford-Clark has been concerned with a three-fold dialectic. On the one hand, religion (and he is here thinking primarily of the Judaeo-Christian and Islamic traditions) has a set of ideas which express a certain type of experience and ideal. These ideas centre upon the conception of a loving and merciful God. On the other hand, however valid the experience of such a Being may be in itself, it is a sad and tragic fact that the creatures whom God supposedly loves are prone to all kinds of disasters – death, their own cruelty to one another, mental and physical disease, and so on. Already there is a tension in human experience, between God's love and created pain. The third element in the dialectic is men's need for reassurance and love. This need has its own nobilities as well as its weaknesses: but is it founded upon illusion? And if there be no higher power, what mainspring of self-sacrifice and concern is left?

The contradiction between religion and life seems inescapable. For the joys of human existence do not exist alone, and the contemplation of evil is enough to turn the intellect away from belief in a good Creator (so it is argued); yet on the other hand religious belief expresses something so deep in the fabric of human psychology that the ideal must be believed in. Dr Stafford-Clark does not elaborate on this, but I imagine that his thesis could be applied with equal force to secular ideologies, and not only to traditional religion.

In opening up this dilemma, Dr Stafford-Clark raises issues which point the way forward. The study of religion must come to grips with and must test historically, comparatively and empirically the springs of religious belief in the human psyche. This task is only begun. Like other scientific enterprises, such as biochemistry, it is recent and late in the history of knowledge. But the year is only 1970. If the world has a future, the human race is still very young. Pointing us along the path is the artistic and pointed figure of human psychology. Dr Stafford-Clark's confrontation between the three arms of his dialectic is an important stimulus for us to go on. Meanwhile we are grateful for the rich way in which he has presented his complex and imaginative theme.

Bibliography

The sources of main quotations only are included in this bibliography; that is, where a section quoted contains reference to other quotations (for example, in the section from Sherrington's *Man on His Nature*), these secondary sources are not separately listed.

CHAPTER 1

Ignaz Maybaum, *Creation and Guilt*, Vallentine, Mitchell, London, 1969.
Aldous Huxley, *The Devils of Loudon*, Chatto & Windus, London, 1952.
Sir Charles Sherrington, *Man on His Nature*, Penguin Books, Harmondsworth, 1955.
Sigmund Freud, *The Future of an Illusion*, standard edition in the *Collected Works*, Hogarth Press and Institute of Psychoanalysis, 1927.
Anon., Hindu hymn.
David Stafford-Clark, *What Freud Really Said*, Macdonald, London, 1965.
David Stafford-Clark, *Autumn Shadow*, Blackwell, Oxford, 1941.
David Stafford-Clark, 'The Way to the Battle', unpublished collection of poetry.

CHAPTER 2

David Stafford-Clark, *What Freud Really Said*, Macdonald, London, 1965.
Rex Warner, *The Cult of Power*, John Lane, The Bodley Head, London, 1946.
Carl Gustav Jung, *Psychology and Religion*, Yale University Press, 1946.
Aldous Huxley, *The Devils of Loudon*, Chatto & Windus, London, 1952.

BIBLIOGRAPHY

C. S. Lewis, *Miracles*, Geoffrey Bles: The Centenary Press, London, 1947.
C. S. Lewis, *Broadcast Talks*, Geoffrey Bles: The Centenary Press, London, 1947.
Milton Rokeach, *The Three Christs of Ypsilanti*, Alfred A. Knopf, New York: Random House, Toronto, 1967.
The Gospel According to St Matthew, 5: 28.
V. H. Mottram, *The Physical Basis of Personality*, Penguin Books Harmondsworth, 1944.
Kenneth Walker, *Meaning and Purpose*, Jonathan Cape, London, 1944.
C. Seaborn Jones, *Treatment of Torture*, Tavistock Publications, London, 1968.
George Bernard Shaw, *Prefaces*, Constable, London, 1934.
David Stafford-Clark, 'The Way to the Battle', unpublished collection of poetry.
T. S. Eliot, *Four Quartets*, Faber & Faber, London, 1944.

CHAPTER 3

Mrs C. S. Alexander, 'There is a Green Hill Far Away', from *Hymns, Ancient and Modern*.
The Gospel According to St Matthew, 10: 29-33.
Joseph Heller, *Catch 22*, Jonathan Cape, London, 1962.
The Gospel According to St Luke, 12: 6 and 7.
George Bernard Shaw, *The Adventures of the Black Girl in Her Search for God*, Constable, London, 1932.
Fyodor Dostoyevsky, *The Brothers Karamazov*, translated by Constance Garnett, Heinemann, London, 1912.
Kurt Vonnegut, *Slaughterhouse 5*, Jonathan Cape, London, 1970.
Herman Melville, *Moby Dick*, Cresset Press, London, 1946.
Peter Shaffer, *The Royal Hunt of the Sun*, Hamish Hamilton, London, 1964.

CHAPTER 4

The Psalms, Psalm 89.
C. G. Jung, *The Answer to Job*, Routledge & Kegan Paul, London, 1952.
Cardinal J. H. Newman, *Lectures on Anglican Difficulties*, 1864.

George Santayana, *Selected Critical Writings*, edited by Norman Henfrey, Cambridge University Press, 1968.
The Book of Ecclesiastes, 3: 11.
General Omar Bradley, in an address to the United Nations (reported in the world's press).
Rex Warner, *The Cult of Power*, John Lane, The Bodley Head, London, 1946.
W. B. Yeats, *Collected Poems*, Macmillan, London, 1963.
Rex Warner, *The Wild Goose Chase*, John Lane, The Bodley Head, London, 1937.
Dr F. R. Barry (former Bishop of Southwark), 'Is God's Judgment Still Viable?', *The Times*, 13 December 1969.
Fyodor Dostoyevsky, *The Possessed*, translated by Constance Garnett, Heinemann, London, 1914.
William Shakespeare, *The Sonnets*, Sonnet 116, Shakespeare Head Press, Oxford, 1947.
George Orwell, *Animal Farm*, Secker & Warburg, London, 1945.
David Stafford-Clark, 'The Psychology of Prejudice and Persecution', the Robert Waley Cohen Lecture given to the Council of Christians and Jews, London, 1960.
A. E. Housman, *More Poems*, Jonathan Cape, London, 1936.
The Book of Ecclesiastes, 3: 11–13.

CHAPTER 5

Herman Melville, *Moby Dick*, Cresset Press, London, 1946.
Peter Shaffer, *The Royal Hunt of the Sun*, Hamish Hamilton, London, 1964.
Peter Medawar, *Induction and Intuition in Scientific Thought*, Methuen, London, 1969.
David Stafford-Clark, *What Freud Really Said*, Macdonald, London, 1965.
David Stafford-Clark, BBC broadcast in 'Lift Up Your Hearts', 12 February 1957.
David Stafford-Clark, *Autumn Shadow*, Blackwell, Oxford, 1941.
A. E. Housman, *More Poems*, Jonathan Cape, London, 1936.

BIBLIOGRAPHY

APPENDIX 1

8-mm. film taken by Abraham Zapruder in Dealey Plaza, Dallas, Texas, 22 November 1963, copyright © Time-Life Inc.

Norman Mailer, *Advertisements for Myself*, André Deutsch, London, 1961.

Frank London, *City Psychiatric*, Four Square Books, London, 1956.

T. S. Naipaul, 'Contribution to Symposium on Violence', *Twentieth Century Magazine*, 1965.

Film: *The Wild Bunch*, with credit sequence: Sam Peckinpah, Warner Bros., Seven Arts, 1969.

APPENDIX 2

George Santayana, *Selected Critical Writings*, edited by Norman Henfrey, Cambridge University Press, 1968.

Sir Charles Sherrington, *Man on His Nature*, Penguin Books, Harmondsworth, 1955.

Gillian Freeman, *The Undergrowth of Literature*, with a Foreword by David Stafford-Clark, Nelson, London, 1967.

David Stafford-Clark, 'Frigidity', *Nova*, January 1966.

David Stafford-Clark, 'Consumer's Guide to Do-it-Yourself Sex', *Nova*, July 1966.

David Stafford-Clark, 'Odious Letters', *Christian Action*, Autumn 1966.

David Stafford-Clark, 'Pornography', *Twentieth Century Magazine*, Summer 1965.

Anthony Storr, *Sexual Deviation*, Penguin Books, Harmondsworth, 1964.

Suzanne Lilar, *Aspects of Love in Western Society*, Thames & Hudson, London, 1965.

APPENDIX 3

Louis Colange, *The Life of the Devil*, Alfred A. Knopf, New York, 1929.

Eric Mapele, *The Domain of Devils*, Robert Hale, London, 1966.

Encyclopedia of Witchcraft and Demonology, edited by R. H. Robins, Peter Nevill, London, 1959.

The Thirty-Nine Articles from the *Book of Common Prayer*, Oxford University Press.
Foxe's Book of Martyrs.
Cardinal J. H. Newman, *Lectures on Anglican Difficulties*, 1864.
Aldous Huxley, *The Devils of Loudon*, Chatto & Windus, London, 1952.

APPENDIX 4

T. S. Eliot, *Four Quartets*, Faber & Faber, London, 1944.
'Palinurus' (Cyril Connolly), *The Unquiet Grave*, Horizon, London, 1944.
David Stafford-Clark, series of articles in *The Times*, 17 February, 11 and 12 April 1967.
Professor Sir Aubrey Lewis, 'Psychological Medicine', sect. XXI in *A Textbook of the Practice of Medicine*, edited by Frederick W. Price, Humphrey Milford, London: Oxford University Press, 6th ed., 1941.
Aldous Huxley, *The Doors of Perception*, Chatto & Windus, London, 1954.

APPENDIX 5

Peter Shaffer, *The Royal Hunt of the Sun*, Hamish Hamilton, London, 1954.
J. E. Orme, *Time, Experience and Behaviour*, Illiffe Books, London, 1969.
The Voices of Time, edited by J. T. Fraser, George Braziller, New York, 1966.
G. J. Whitrow, *The Natural Philosophy of Time*, Nelson, London, 1961.
L. A. Khalfin, paper in *Journal of Experimental Physics*, vol. 39, 1960, pp. 504–6.
H. A. C. Dobbs, 'A Time to Every Purpose', *Para-psychology*, New York, 1967.
David Stafford-Clark, 'Current Theories on Conscience and Consciousness', *Proceedings of Royal Institution*, Elsevier Publishing, 1970 (in press).

David Stafford-Clark, 'Reflections on Time and Consciousness', broadcast on BBC Third Programme, 18 September 1969.

Minkowski, Address to the 18th Assembly of German Natural Scientists and Physicians, Cologne, 21 September 1908.

APPENDIX 6

Tim Hardin, 'If I Were a Carpenter', song published by the Faithfull Virtue Music Co., New York, 1966.

David Stafford-Clark, Address to the Commonwealth Foundation, London, Autumn 1968.

Hugh Montefiore, *The Question Mark*, Collins, London, 1969.